ST MARY-AT-HILL

Carved Panel on Organ Front

The Parish Church of ST MARY-AT-HILL *in the City of London*

by

PAUL JEFFERY, CBE, PHD

with appendices by
Richard Lea & Bruce Watson

THE ECCLESIOLOGICAL SOCIETY
1996

Above:
WOODWORK AT THE ENTRANCE TO THE NAVE.

On title page:
DEATH'S HEAD OVER SOUTH PASSAGE DOOR

First published 1996

The Ecclesiological Society
St Andrew-by-the-Wardrobe
Queen Victoria Street
London EC4V 5DE

Printed by the Doppler Press, Brentwood, Essex

ISBN 0 946823 11 1

CONTENTS

LIST OF LINE ILLUSTRATIONS

RECONSTRUCTION DRAWINGS

The reconstruction drawings are at the rear of the book, on page 71 and following.

TAILPIECES AND OTHER UNATTRIBUTED LINE DRAWINGS

The tailpieces and other unattributed line drawings are taken from Mark Rogers, *Down Thames Street,* (1921), with the exception of those on pages 57 and 64 which are reproduced from prints held by the Guildhall Library, Corporation of London, by kind permission.

LIST OF PLATES

Plates will be found at the centre of the book

SOURCES OF ILLUSTRATIONS

We are grateful to the following for permission to reproduce illustrations: The British Architectural Library, Royal Institute of British Architects, London (Figs 7, 8 and 9); English Heritage (Plates 6*b* and 14*a*; the reconstruction drawings); Guildhall Prints and Manuscripts Collection, Guildhall Library, Corporation of London (Plates 1, 2*a*, 2*b*, 2*c*, 5, 7, 9*b*, 10*a*, 15*b*, 16*a*, and 16*b*; Fig. 5; tailpieces on pages 57 and 64; illustration on front cover); *The Independent*/Geraint Lewis (Plate 12*b*); the National Monuments Record at the Royal Commission on the Historical Monuments of England (Plates 3, 4, 6*a*, 8, 9*a*, 10*b*, 11*a*, 11*b*, 12*a*, and 13). Fig. 3 was produced for this volume by Paul Jeffery. Figs 10 and 11 were created by Bruce Watson, and have previously been reproduced in *London and Middlesex Archaeological Society Trans.*, (1992), 43, pp. 192–200.

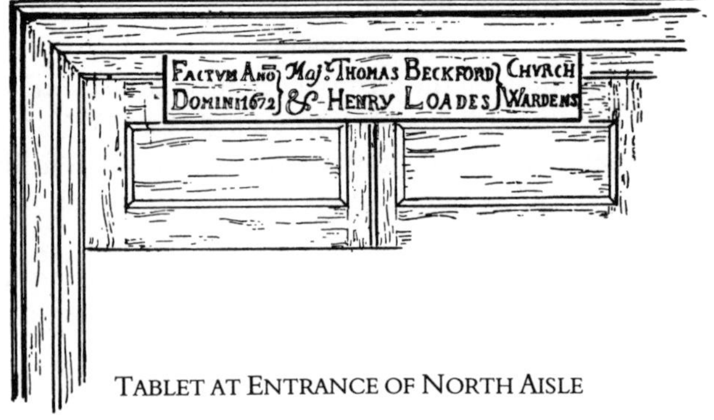

TABLET AT ENTRANCE OF NORTH AISLE

AUTHOR'S ACKNOWLEDGEMENTS

I am grateful to all those who have helped in the compilation of this monograph, including John Barnes, architect for the restoration of the church; librarians and archivists of the Guildhall Library who, as always, have been most helpful in locating and producing documentary sources and illustrative material; Stephen Humphrey for research on the possible connection of the church with Thomas Becket; Robert Crayford for illuminating discussions, particularly those concerning eighteenth century joinery; Paul Velluet and English Heritage, London Division for access to unpublished material; and particularly Richard Lea for his reconstruction drawings of the church, all reproduced by kind permission of English Heritage, London Division. I am also grateful to Bruce Watson for his appendix summarising the archaeology of the church.

Shield at Entrance to Choir

A Word *to the* Visitor

THE FIRST IMPRESSION of St Mary-at-Hill is now one of spaciousness, enhanced by the removal of the pews following the fire of 1988. The absence of arcades dividing the church into a nave and aisles supports the impression of the building as an auditory, a large single-celled room, in which the high ceiling and roof, supported on four Composite columns arranged in a square, and the hemispherical dome combine with the tall, round-headed windows to emphasise the essential unity of the enclosed space.

Surprisingly, this unity is derived, not from any preconceived design, but by a process of evolution lasting four centuries.

The lower parts of the north and south walls of the church remain from the late-mediaeval rebuilding. The upper parts of all the walls are from the Wren period. The tower and western vestibules are from Gwilt's rebuilding of 1787–8, and the ceiling and dome are by Savage, 1826–7.

The recent restoration has left the building much as it was before the fire of 1988, but the furniture and many of the fittings have still to be returned.

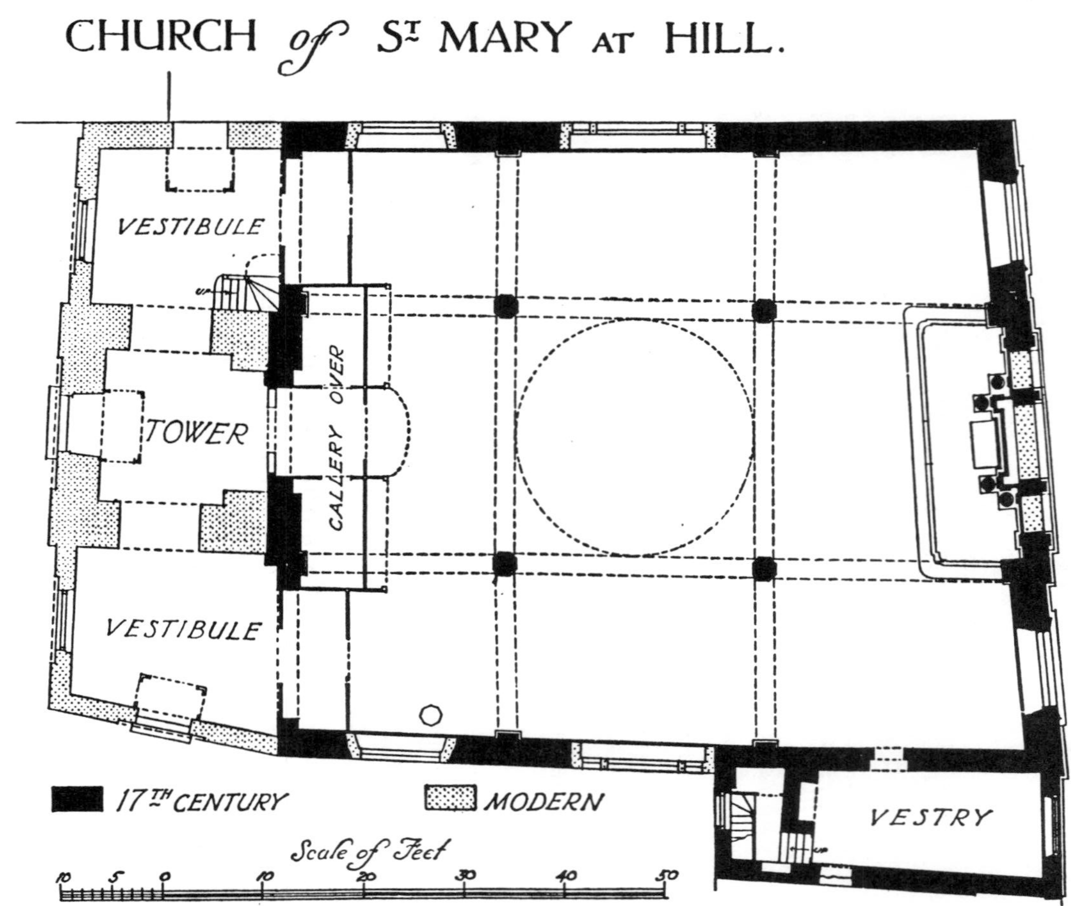
CHURCH of ST MARY AT HILL.
VESTIBULE
TOWER
VESTIBULE
GALLERY OVER
VESTRY
17TH CENTURY
MODERN
Scale of Feet
10 5 0 10 20 30 40 50

INTRODUCTION

IN the early part of the seventeenth century the City of London was a densely populated area. It was divided into over a hundred parishes, each with its own church, most of which were in existence by the end of the twelfth century. Of these eighty-six were destroyed in the Great Fire of London, September 1666. Only fifty-one were rebuilt, all before the end of the century, under the general direction of Sir Christopher Wren. Since that time, catastrophe of one sort or another has reduced their numbers to twenty-one, with a little over half remaining as parish churches. Some are inevitably under threat as the City Archdeaconry recognises that fewer places for worship are required and reorganises to meet the needs of the twenty-first century.

At the time of writing St Mary-at-Hill remains a parish church. Despite the irregularities of its structure it is a fine building, with some of the fabric surviving from mediaeval times [*see reconstruction drawings following page 71*]. It is one of the few to escape extensive reordering in Victorian times and, although scarred, to survive largely intact after two world wars. Until the 1988 fire, it was the only

---

Fig. 1 (opposite) *Plan of the church, produced by the Royal Commission on Historical Monuments in 1929.*

church in the City to retain its box pews. The church retained much of its nineteenth century atmosphere, redolent partly of Wren and partly of Dickens, contrasting vividly with some of the post-war restorations. Above all, it amply demonstrates that the changes of over three hundred years can successfully be accommodated in a building of this quality. With such as this, there can be no excuse for demolition. Its loss, following the fire of May 1988, would have been a major tragedy and a set-back to all those determined to preserve what is still left of the City of London as it was before wartime bombing and the destructive rebuilding of the late twentieth century.

Our knowledge of the history of St Mary-at-Hill, as that of most of the City churches, is based partly upon an examination of the fabric of the building, partly upon a study of original documents that happen to have survived and partly upon what historians have told us. John Stow, ?1525–1605, has provided an invaluable record of the early history: his account of the church, based upon what he saw, what he read and what he was told, is of a building already centuries old. His account was followed by that of others, notably Strype, Hatton, Maitland, Allen, Birch – historians, topographers, ecclesiologists and others who described the church and its fittings. What they saw and recorded is the main and sometimes only record of what is no longer there for us to see.

The fire of 1988, destructive as it was, nevertheless provided an opportunity to take a closer look at the fabric of the building. Traces of earlier buildings on the site were found and recorded, and the limited excavation below the church floor added to our knowledge of the changes to the site over more than eight hundred years. The reconstruction of any historic building after a major fire brings not only the need to know more about what the fire has left but also more about what has been destroyed. St Mary-at-Hill was no exception. It was this need that prompted the compilation of these notes.

THE HISTORY OF THE CHURCH

The Setting of the Church

WITH a dozen or so of the mediaeval parish churches of the City dedicated to the Blessed Virgin Mary it was by far the most popular dedication in London, as elsewhere, reflecting the importance of the Virgin as a cult figure in early mediaeval times. As with almost all the parish churches of London, each of these St Marys had a subsidiary name reflecting the precise location, the name of the patron, donor or benefactor, or even perhaps an attribute by which the church could be distinguished from the others of the same dedication – hence such names as St Mary-le-Bow, St Mary Somerset, St Mary Aldermanbury and St Mary-at-Hill. The latter is apparently named from its position on the steep slope of the hill above [Plates 1 and 3]. In early documents it is referred to with a variety of names including St Mary de Hyll, St Mary atte Hulle and Sanctae Maria apud Montem.[1]

The church occupies a site on the hill between the river Thames and Thames Street to the south, and Eastcheap to the north, fronting a street also and somewhat confusingly known as St Mary-at-Hill to the east and Lovat Lane (formerly Rope Lane, Lucas Lane, then Love

Lane)[2] to the west [*Fig. 2*]. These two streets are linked by a narrow, paved passageway which now occupies the full length of the south side of the building. In mediaeval times this gave access to the church through a door in the middle of the south side and to a churchyard which was then to the south of the church.

The church as it now stands neither dominates the surrounding buildings nor is dominated by them; it remains in scale with a part of London that has so far largely escaped the worst of London's post-war development [Plate 4].

The Early Mediaeval Church

The date when the church was first built, like that of so many others in the City of London, is not recorded. The earliest reference so far found is from the twelfth century when, at some time before 1195, Walter de Gaunt, first Abbot of Waltham after the re-foundation of the Abbey by Henry II in 1177, purchased ground on the south side of the church of St Mary-at-Hill. He used this to build a mansion for his accommodation and that of his successors whenever they visited London.[3] Richard, the fifth Abbot, obtained a licence from William de Sancta Maria, Bishop of London 1199–1221, with the assent of the Chapter of St Paul's Cathedral, to celebrate divine service in a chapel which he built in a court near the church of St Mary-at-Hill.[4] All oblations made to this chapel were to be transferred to the church of St Mary-at-Hill. Thomas Becket was named by Stow as a 'person'

Fig. 2 (opposite) *Detail from the Leake and Hollar map of 1667 (c. 17½ inches to the mile), showing the devastation after the Great Fire. St Mary-at-Hill church (no. 87) lies between Love Lane and St Mary Hill. St Andrew Hubbard lies to the north west of St Mary-at-Hill, unnumbered, and St George, Botolph Lane due west (no. 86); St Botolph, Billingsgate (no. 85) is to the south of St George's. St Margaret Patten (no. 89) lies slightly east of north of St Mary-at-Hill, and St Gabriel, Fenchurch Street (unnumbered) somewhat further in the same direction. All these churches in Billingsgate ward were destroyed in the Fire. For their subsequent history see page 56.*

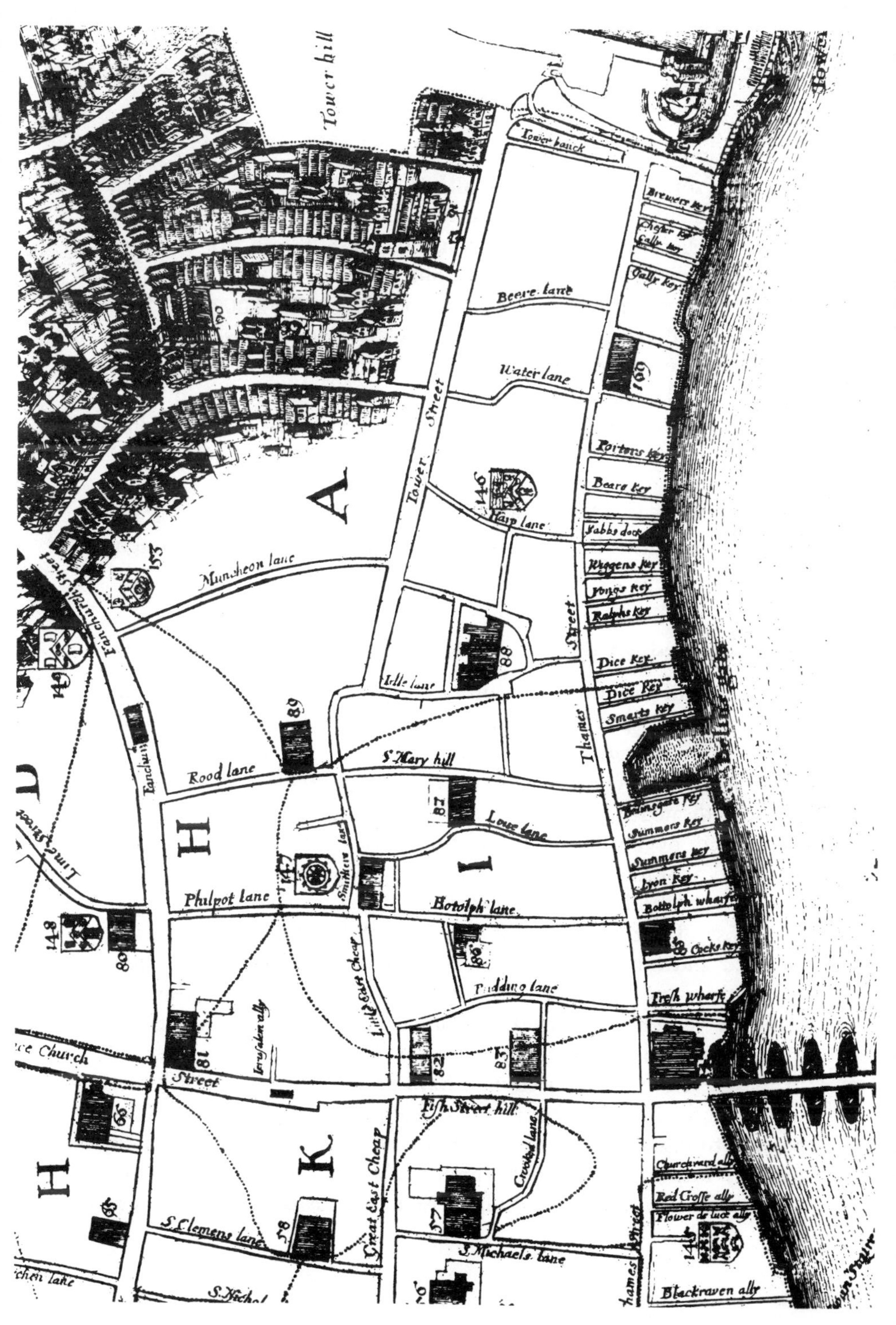

Tower hill
Tower banck
Brewers key
Chester key
Gally key
Beere lane
Water lane
Porters key
Beare key
Harp lane
Wiggens key
Yongs key
Ralphs key
Dice key
Dice key
Smarts key
Muncheon lane
Tower Street
Thames Street
Rood lane
S.t Mary hill
Idle lane
Love lane
Philpot lane
Botolph lane
Summers key
Lyon key
Bottolph wharfe
Cocks key
Pudding lane
Fresh wharfe
Little East Cheap
Jerusalem ally
Fish Street hill
Crooked lane
Great East Cheap
S. Clemens lane
S. Michaels lane
Churchyard ally
Red Crosse ally
Flower de luce ally
Blackraven ally

(i.e. a 'parson') of St Mary-at-Hill, which suggests that the church was in existence in the middle part of the twelfth century, giving a slightly earlier date for the church, but the authority for Becket's association with St Mary-at-Hill is doubtful.[5]

Some of the mediaeval churches of London are known to have been founded as private chapels and to have then consisted of no more than a small and simple nave and chancel. Neither written nor archaeological evidence is known in support of such an origin for St Mary-at-Hill and the foundations of an early mediaeval building revealed in excavation within the church in 1991 [*see Appendix A*] are those of a large and substantial building with nave, north aisle and chancel.[6] This building apparently occupied a major part of the present site, extending almost if not completely to the present west wall.

The Late Mediaeval Church: 1487–1666

By the end of the fifteenth century it was the largest church in the Ward of Billingsgate, containing four chapels. Those dedicated to St Stephen (on the north side) and St Katharine (or Catharine) on the south joined the choir. St Anne's chapel was enclosed by screens. Those dedicated to St Catherine, St Anne and St Christopher were maintained by brotherhoods of the parish and there were altars dedicated to St Mary, St Edmund the King, St John the Baptist and St Thomas – probably Thomas Becket.

Most of the churches in the City of London were repaired, enlarged and rebuilt at intervals throughout the mediaeval period. Very little is known of such attention to the fabric of St Mary-at-Hill until the year 1487, when a substantial rebuilding programme was initiated, beginning with the north aisle. This rebuilding is recorded in the surviving parish accounts. Bays or arches on the north side were paid for by a number of individual parishioners in 1490.[7] John Smart promised an arch as did John Holbed and John Duckling together with Alderman John Plummer. William Prewne promised a whole arch or a window and Harry Kello what is usually assumed to have been a large arch and which may have marked the position of the cross aisle or transepts. These transepts did not extend beyond the outer walls and there is no evidence for them in Wenceslaus Hollar's panoramas of 1647 and 1666 [Plates *2b* and *2c*] which show the south side of the church.[8] They may have been covered by the same lean-to roof as the rest of the aisles and been no more than an internal arrangement of the space, derived from the earlier mediaeval church and dividing the sanctuary and chapels from the nave. Nevertheless, their presence indicates a church of some pretension.

The fabric of the north wall of the late mediaeval church, revealed in repairs undertaken at the western end in 1984, shows no signs of any corbelling nor other evidence to indicate that the aisles were vaulted, enabling Richard Lea to conclude that the aisle was timber roofed.[9] The repairs revealed the remains of two of the late mediaeval windows corresponding to a bay width of 4.46m (14ft 7in) which, in the wall of 87 feet, suggests that there were six bays to the north aisle, although not necessarily all with windows [*Figs 3a and R1–R3*]. The south aisle of the late mediaeval church would, no doubt similarly have had six bays, as shown in Hollar's print of 1647.[10] The south aisle, whose rebuilding was begun in the year 1500, was originally shorter than the north but was lengthened in the rebuilding by incorporating the area now occupied by the south-west lobby and probably also the western end of the south aisle which had formerly been the site of the Abbot of Waltham's kitchen. For this land the churchwardens paid a quit-rent to the Abbot which, after the Dissolution, was paid to the Crown.

Hollar's views show also three tall structures resembling chimney stacks along the south wall, rising above the parapet. One of these may have been an external turret giving access to the roof. Turret staircases are known to have existed in a number of the mediaeval City churches, but few survived rebuilding after the Great Fire.[11] They may originally have given access also to the rood loft. The other structures may have been chimneys, with that at the eastern end coming from the vestry. What was almost certainly a flue and chimney in a position between the third and fourth bays of the south wall, shown in an engraving by Coney and Skelton of 1814 [Plate 16*a*],[12] may date from 1765–6 when open stoves provided the first form of heating for the church.

The rebuilding of the aisles was followed by a rebuilding of the tower, and the church was re-dedicated in 1503–4. At that time the church consisted of a nave with north and south aisles extending the full length of the church from the street called St Mary-at-Hill to what is now Lovat Lane. The nave was lit from a clerestory and was separated from the aisles by arches supported upon columns or piers. The position of the transepts or cross aisle has not been firmly established, although it may be inferred from the doorways occupying positions in the centre of the north and south walls, that it too was in the centre of the church.

The plan shown in *Fig. 3a* is a reconstruction of the 1487–1500 church. Surviving features of the late mediaeval church, revealed by the removal of the wainscoting from the present building following the fire of 1988, include the original jambs of the north and south doors and ashlar masonry set in the rubble of the south wall. The plan does not show the vestry which, from an early date, was attached to the east end of the south wall. The rectory occupied (as it does now) the next plot down the hill.

The tower, at a slight angle to the rest of the church, and therefore most likely aligned to Lovat Lane, intruded into the body of the church with the aisles carried past it to the west. Hollar's view of 1647 [Plate 2*b*] shows that the tower was crenellated and capped with a low pyramidal roof, presumably lead-covered. The main walls of the church may also have been crenellated, although this detail is difficult to confirm from the print. The aisles, at a lower height than the nave, were lit from wide, pointed, arched windows of late Perpendicular style with hood mouldings. The church was partly

---

Fig. 3 (opposite) *Three stages in the development of the church. Note changes to arcades, wall openings and tower: (a) Late mediaeval (reconstruction); (b) as rebuilt 1670–74 (reconstruction); and (c) after Savage's work of 1826–7.*

a.

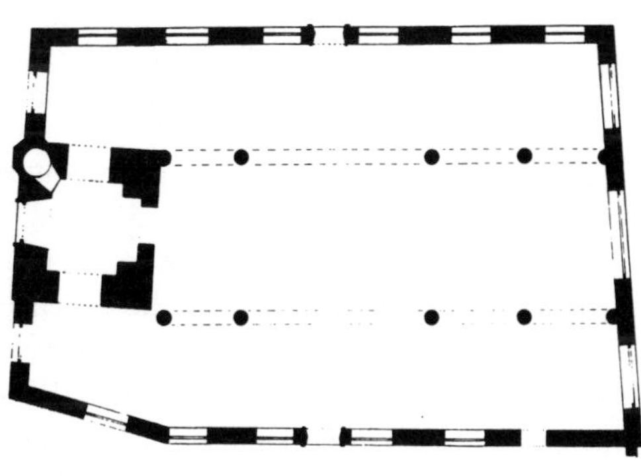

b.

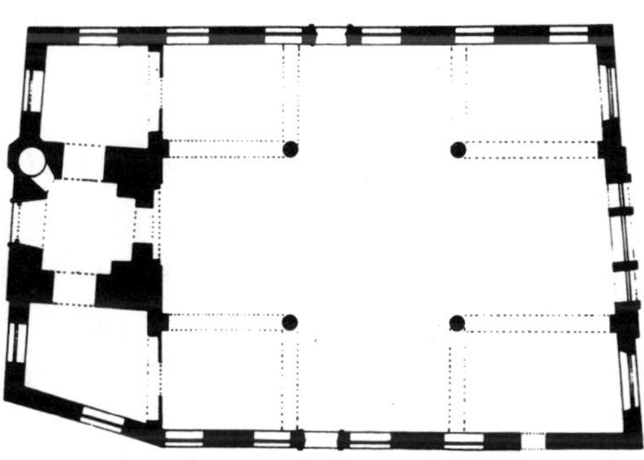

c.

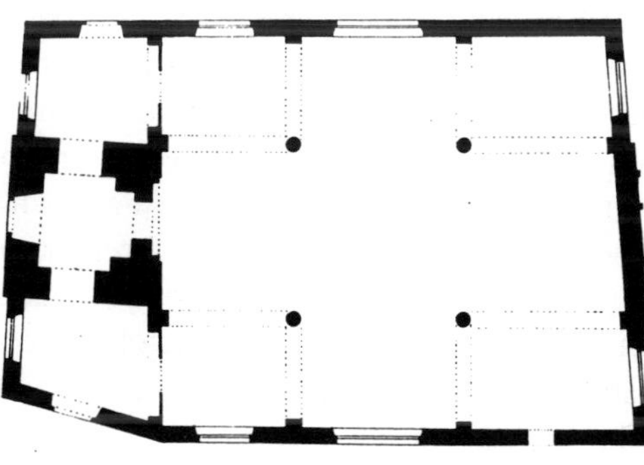

paved with tiles and had a number of gravestones set in the floor. It was covered with a timber roof partly leaded and partly tiled.

An inventory of 1553 lists six bells, including the Sanctus or 'Saints' bell, all of which were lost in the Great Fire. This inventory also records that the church at that time had two organs, one larger than the other. A new wooden pulpit had been provided for the church and a new rood constructed with attendant figures of St Mary and St John, replacing an older rood sold in 1509–10. The new rood was taken down in 1559, early in the reign of Elizabeth I.

This late mediaeval church was repaired and renovated in 1616.

The Parish Recovers from the Great Fire: 1668–1670

The church suffered badly in the Great Fire of September 1666. The timber roof, floors of the tower and all combustible furnishings and fittings, including any that may have survived from before the Reformation, were all consumed. The building was badly damaged but not completed destroyed. The church, in its ruined state, is shown in Hollar's 'post-Fire' engraving of London with its roof apparently missing but tower and walls substantially complete [Plate 2*c*]. It was from this shell that the church was reconstructed.

It was not until 1668 that life in the parish of St Mary-at-Hill resumed any kind of normality. The first vestry minute concerned with the church is dated 21 July 1668 when the churchwardens, vestrymen and 'other skilful workmen' were ordered to view the church and steeple and report.[13] In August, needing more expert advice, the vestry ordered that the churchwardens should get 'Mr Jerman' (Edward Jarman, City Surveyor) and some other able workmen to view the church. On 7 October it considered a report by Jarman and 'Mr Yonge' (Nicholas Young, mason) concerning the preservation of the church, steeple and walls. A committee was then appointed to contract and bargain with workmen to secure the walls and steeple as recommended in the survey, while at a meeting of the committee held on 12 May 1670 it was agreed that money should be raised for the 'speedy rebuilding and restoring the church and vestry house'. It is clear from these records that, since a substantial part of the fabric remained after the Fire, the vestrymen intended to use it to restore the building to its original form. In this they were doing no more than following the advice of Edward Jarman and Nicholas Young and what was being done elsewhere in the City, including at St Sepulchre and St Vedast, Foster Lane.

The extent and nature of the work done is not recorded but, as the largest payment was to Robert Harris, carpenter and as later, in 1671, another carpenter, Richard Lock, was paid for moving the belfry floor, it can be inferred that, in addition to securing the walls, work was done to restore the internal structure of the tower with its floors and stairways. In 1669 approval was given for Harris to be paid one half of his bill for carpentry, but in the absence of parish accounts for this period, it is not known if this payment was made or deferred. Further sums expended by the parish were paid by Dr Christopher Wren (he was not knighted until 1673), as follows: [14]

	£	*s.*	*d.*
James Florey, *mason*	6.	8.	0
Thomas Norfolke, *bricklayer*	5.	0.	0
Robert Harris, *carpenter*	170.	7.	6
Anthony Ives, *smith*	12.	0.	0
Labouring	29.	19.	6
TOTAL	*£223.*	*15.*	*0*

Had they been left to themselves, the vestry would have had difficulty in raising the sum needed to complete the restoration and the work would undoubtedly have proceeded slowly. Fortunately for the parish, following the passing of the Act of 1670,[15] the task of restoring the church was assumed by the Commissioners appointed for the rebuilding of fifty one churches of the City of London (the Archbishop of Canterbury, Bishop of London and Lord Mayor of London). The rebuilding programme was to be financed by a tax upon coal coming into the Port of London. Wren was appointed to act in what would now be described as an executive capacity to the Commissioners, with responsibility for getting the churches rebuilt in accordance with their decisions.

Even in the early days after the fire it had been recognised that not all the eighty-six churches destroyed would need to be rebuilt and that there was a strong case for some form of grouping of the parishes. A proposal of 1667 would have promoted the union of St Mary-at-Hill with St George, Botolph Lane,[16] but this was abandoned in 1670 in favour of union with St Andrew Hubbard. The rebuilt church of St Mary-at-Hill, with a single incumbent, was to serve both parishes with joint services. Expenses in connection with the repair and upkeep of the church were to be shared in an agreed ratio, one third contributed by St Andrew Hubbard and two thirds by St Mary-at-Hill, reflecting the greater size and hence greater income from rates of the latter parish. In most other respects the two parishes continued as separate entities, each preserving its own vested interests, maintaining a corporate existence with separate vestry, separate administration and separate accounts. The arrangement was to be a source of friction, disagreement and acrimony between the two parishes over a number of what now seem to be rather trivial matters – such as the use of doors to the church, a matter settled by the parishioners of St Mary-at-Hill using the north and south doors, those of St Andrew the door beneath the tower. Other disputes were over burial rights and the procedure to be used for choosing a new church organist.

Rebuilding of St Mary-at-Hill: 1670–1674

The Act of 1670 specified that the churches to be rebuilt should be erected according to such models and of such dimensions and in such manner and form as the Commissioners (with his Majesty's approbation) should direct. Few designs are known positively to have been submitted to Charles II,[17] but this wording was reflected in the decision of the Commissioners at their first meeting, held on 13 June 1670:

Dr Christopher Wren, Surveyor General of his Majesty's Works, Mr Robert Hooke and Mr Edward Woodroffe are hereby required to repair forthwith the aforesaid churches and take an account of the extent of the parishes, the sites of the churches, the state and conditions of the ruins and accordingly prepare fit models and draughts to be presented for his Majesty's approbation . . .[18]

The 'aforesaid churches' referred to a list of fifteen selected as the first to be rebuilt or repaired. The selection was made, in part at least, from those parishes that had already made some move towards repairing or restoring their own churches and included St Mary-at-Hill.

It soon became apparent that the rate at which the rebuilding of fifty parish churches could proceed greatly exceeded the rate at which money derived from the coal tax accumulated to pay for them and, on 13 July, the Commissioners agreed that 'those churches that will advance present money shall begin to build'. Although this scheme is believed to have originated from a deposit made by the parish of St Edmund the King, one of the first deposits was from St Mary-at-Hill.[19] This was £500, paid in July 1670, with a further £500 in November 1670. Sums totalling £1000 were paid by September 1671 and a further £500 in March 1673. All deposits were eventually repaid to the parish. It may be concluded that the vestry was desperately anxious not to lose its place in the building programme and to ensure that there was no slackening in the pace of building.

Credit for the design of the church of St Mary-at-Hill is generally given to Wren. In the sense that he was responsible under the Commissioners for the completion of the church, it is right and proper that it should be recorded as a work undertaken under his direction, or as recorded in *Parentalia*,[20] under his 'care and conduct'. It is however now clear that he could not *personally* have drawn up plans and supervised the construction of about fifty parish churches at the same time as designing and building St Paul's Cathedral and attending to his many other duties as Surveyor of his Majesty's Works. With regard to St Mary-at-Hill, no record has so far been found to indicate who was the author of the design. The Commissioners' order noted above indicates that it was their intention that the design of the churches should be shared by Wren, Hooke and Woodroffe. Evidence for Woodroffe's involvement in this activity is slim, but there is abundant evidence for designing by Robert Hooke. He was a professor at Gresham College in Bishopsgate, where he lived, and must have known the eastern part of the City well. As one of the three surveyors appointed after the Fire to set out the plots of land for rebuilding he was responsible for measuring the sites in the eastern part of the City.[21] The parish of St Mary-at-Hill owned property which had been burnt in the Fire, and by 1670 would have had dealings with Hooke over their property boundaries. The possibility that Hooke may have been the author of the design for their church cannot be ignored although it is recognised that the frequent meetings between him and Wren would have ensured that the design evolved to the satisfaction of both men. A collaboration between them may have been how many of the churches, including St Mary-at-Hill, were designed.

The mason's contract for rebuilding the east front is dated 1 November 1670 and the carpenter's for a new ceiling 2 December.[22] It may therefore be inferred that by the end of 1670 the general design of the church had been settled. The decision was made to retain what was left of the north and south walls of the church and to provide a new internal wall to the east of the tower, creating two small rooms at the west end. This wall reduced the size of the church by one bay which, since the rebuilt church would need to accommodate also the parishioners of St Andrew Hubbard, must indicate that the mediaeval building had been far larger than needed for St Mary-at-Hill parish.

In the rebuilding, shown in plan in *Fig. 3b*, the still standing north and south walls, constructed largely of stone rubble, were repaired and carried to a new height, shown in the reconstruction [*Figs R4 and R5*]. The Perpendicular windows of these fronts were left and probably also the hood mouldings for them, although these were later stripped when the walls were stuccoed. The doorways in the centre of both north and south fronts were also left, but a new north doorcase was provided by Joshua Marshall, mason, who carved a 'death's head' for it.[23] This is now over the east end of the passageway to the south of the church [*illustration on title page*].

The east front contains no work earlier than 1670–74 as the old, late mediaeval east wall was totally demolished. It has changed much since Wren's time. There is no contemporary description, but its appearance can be inferred from the building accounts. The new wall provided the most public aspect of the building and was accordingly the most decorated. Although now stuccoed, it is of stone and the stone work was originally exposed. The centre bay is broken forward and all three bays quoined. Stone work exposed during the reconstruction following the fire of 1988 suggests that the cornice was broken and the pediment enlivened with a circular window, as shown in the reconstruction [*Fig. R6*]. The centre window was mullioned and transomed, and the windows of the outer bays similarly divided [*Fig.* R7].

The building accounts indicate that Joshua Marshall provided decoration in the form of three festoons totalling 57 feet in length, almost certainly for the east front. Although none are shown in any of the existing views of the church, in the recent repairs the upper part of this wall was stripped of much of its cement rendering revealing tool marks over the outer windows where two of the festoons were chiselled away. There were no such markings above the central window. The remaining festoon can only have been across the central bay and as there would seem to have been insufficient room for it above the central window, it may have been across the panel below. The festoons may have disappeared in the changes made to the east front by Savage in 1826–7, but are more likely to have been removed earlier. The vestry minutes contain no reference to this and no explanation has so far been found for this destruction.

The festoons are listed in Joshua Marshall's contract for the east front dated 1 November 1670, together with the four capitals for the window which are still in place, and two urns. His bill for the work done includes both the festoons and the capitals, but not the urns, suggesting that, despite their inclusion in the contract, they were omitted in the final design.

The greatest uncertainty in the study of the building as it was constructed in 1670–74 is in respect of its roof. The Savage rebuilding of 1826–7 completely destroyed the earlier structure, but its roof lines, across the backs of the pediments at both the eastern and western ends of the church, were revealed following the fire of 1988 and show that it was of shallower pitch. No indication was found of any seventeenth century pediment to the north or south front.

Related to the roof structure is the internal arrangement of the building. Changes made in the early part of the nineteenth century, including the creation of barrel vaults along and across the building, have tended to give emphasis to the cross axes [Plate 5]. It is fashionable to note the resemblance of St Mary-at-Hill (in particular the internal arrangement of columns and intersecting vaults), to St Martin, Ludgate and St Anne and St Agnes, a Dutch model having been suggested, but it must not be forgotten that at St Mary-at-Hill, these cross axes (or 'transepts') derive from the late mediaeval building. Moreover, the only surviving illustration, from the book of contracts, of the original intention for the 1670–74 ceiling indicates that the main beams provided a wall-to-wall support, and were not broken at the four columns.[24] Although perhaps originally intended, the construction did not follow this sketch. The earliest description of the ceiling is by Hatton and dated 1708:

> the inside thereof, over the middle Ile, is a little arching, in the middle whereof is a handsome Cupilo. The roofs of the side Iles are flat, and the lowest at the four angles, supported with 4 Columns . . .[25]

The only known representation of the ceiling as it may have been at this time is that shown in a drawing from the Crace Collection [Plate 16*b*],[26] made prior to the alterations of 1826–7 by Savage, but without the decorations of the shallow dome described by Hatton as 'Cherubims, Arches and Leaves'. The ceiling was apparently coved to all four walls.

The excavations of 1991 showed that the four columns supporting the roof were positioned roughly, but not exactly, upon the line of earlier foundation walls, now represented, in part at least, by chalk blocks below the floor level. These foundations may also have supported the late mediaeval piers, although no trace of them or their bases was found.

The capitals of the present columns [Plate *6b*] have given rise to much comment. Hatton describes them and the pilasters at the east and west ends of the church as 'of no Order at all, but a Specie partly composed of the Doric and Corinthian'. They are described also as of 'the workmen's own invention',[27] for which there is no authority. Birch described them as 'nondescript . . . but . . . very good and effective',[28] Elizabeth and Wayland Young say that they are by Savage and freely copied from the Tower of the Four Winds at Athens,[29] whilst Malcolm said that they were 'of a strange order'.[30] Pevsner described them as Corinthian,[31] Rogers as Doric[32] and the RCHME as pseudo-classical.[33] They are in fact a Composite capital employing elements from the Doric, Ionic and Corinthian Orders, and are described in Sebastian Serlio's *The Five Books of Architecture*, Book IV [*Fig. 4*]. Wren's library contained a copy of Serlio and it may be presumed that this or another copy would have been available also to Hooke. What is surprising is not that this form of Composite capital should be used, (it is indeed an appropriate form for the four principal columns) but that it does not seem to have been more widely employed, although something similar was used for the peristyle of the steeple of St Mary-le-Bow. The suggestion that Wren was too busy to bother with such detail as this which could be left to the knowledge and skill of the craftsmen, although repeated from book to book on the supposed evidence of this capital, can no longer be entertained.

Fig. 4 *Drawing of composite capital, based on one shown in Sebastian Serlio,* The Five Books of Architecture, *Book IV. The original drawing shows the right hand half of the capital only, and for the diagram above a mirror image has been created to provide the left hand half. Compare Plate 6b.*

The costs of reconstructing the church in the period 1670–74 are given in the building accounts:[34]

	£	s.	d.
Joshua Marshall, *mason*	1928.	1.	2
Thomas Lock, *carpenter*	559.	3.	9
William Cleere, *joiner*	26.	0.	0
John George, *plumber*	810.	1.	4½
George Drew, *smith*	129.	13.	6½
John Grove, *plasterer*	219.	17.	2
John Ayliffe, *glazier*	54.	14.	0
Margaret Pearce, *painter*	29.	6.	3
TOTAL	*£3756.*	*17.*	*3*

This total may be compared with the figure usually given for the rebuilding St Mary-at-Hill of £3980. 12*s*. 3*d*, which represents the craftsmen's bills for 1668–70 and 1670–74, but not that for 1694–5. The total payment from the revenue of the coal tax in respect of this church for all three periods amounted to £5137. 2*s*. 8*d*.

Repairs and Changes: 1679–1695

In 1679 the churchwardens reported that rain water from the roof came down the east front, as presumably it must have done since the completion of the church in 1674. Pipes were then provided to conduct the rain water to the ground and rain water heads installed to gather the rain water from the roof. These carry the date 1679 together with the initials SMH (St Mary-at-Hill) and SAH (St Andrew Hubbard).

Surprisingly, the vestry minutes from the end of the century are silent on further problems then being experienced with the building, recorded in the rebuilding accounts[35]. There is a brief comment dated 23 November 1694 when it was reported 'our Church at this present tyme is under Repair at the Publick Charge'. This was a time when most of the churches patched up soon after the Fire were finding that the fabric at the top of the towers was disintegrating, requiring major repair. In the Great Fire the towers tended to act as chimneys, with greater damage to the stonework at the top than had been appreciated. St Mary-at-Hill was no exception.

The opportunity was also taken to make a number of other changes and repairs.[36] The lantern from the tower was removed to enable major repair work to be undertaken at the top of the tower and a new lead-covered timber lantern erected. Early eighteenth century views [*Fig. 5*] show the tower as balustraded, without corner pinnacles but the lantern, probably octagonal, having a bell-shaped cap.

Fig. 5 *An early eighteenth century view of the west end and tower of the church, after the repairs and changes of 1679–95, before Gwilt's rebuilding of 1787. (Print, Guildhall Library, Corporation of London.)*

The changes made to the church at the end of the seventeenth century include the cement rendering of the outside walls of both church and tower. The mullions of the mediaeval windows were repaired and a new outer door and doorcase of oak with pilasters and carved capitals provided for the south door. The church was also redecorated. The costs were as follows:

	£	*s.*	*d.*
Christopher Kempster, *mason*	143.	12.	11
Abraham Wilkins, *carpenter*	326.	15.	8
Matthew Roberts, *plumber*	270.	14.	4

Thomas Colbourn, *smith*	28.	11.	9
Robert Rowland, *coppersmith*	10.	8.	0
Henry Doogood, *plasterer*	294.	14.	10
John Ayliffe, *glazier*	26.	6.	3
William Thompson, *painter*	55.	6.	8
TOTAL	*£1156.*	*10.*	*5*

The blocking of the east window: 1767

The construction of the reredos [Plate 10*a*] obscured much of the light from the east window and in 1767 the vestry decided to block it, although the reason given is hardly credible:

Whereas it appears unto this Vestry that the window in the East End of the Church behind the Altar piece is very unsecure against accidents that may happen by Fire, For securing of which and preserving the Church against any such accidents It is ordered that the said window be Bricked up with a nine inch wall and that the glass be taken out.[37]

Whatever the cause, this bricking up preserved the earlier construction of the window as installed in 1670–72 with mullions and transom dividing it, as shown in Shepherd's undated engraving of about 1831 [Plate 15*b*], and in a print by Billings and Le Keux [*Fig. 6*], published in 1839. [*See also illustration on front cover.*] An examination of the round-headed windows in the north and south bays of the east front has revealed patches of rough stone work to the jambs, suggesting that these windows too were originally divided with mullions and transoms.

Rebuilding of the Tower and West End: 1787–1788

On 8 May 1787 George Gwilt, surveyor to the parish, recommended the rebuilding of the 'steeple' (i.e. the tower) in stone, a rebuilding of the west end [Plate 4], replacement of the lead roof of the church and a partial rebuilding of the south front.[38] In the event,

Fig. 6 *The east front of the church in the early middle years of last century. (Engraving, G. Godwin & J. Britton,* The Churches of London, *1839.)*

the parish decided that, to reduce the cost, the tower would be in brick rather than stone [Plate 16*a*; *Fig.* 7]. As the work proceeded other changes were introduced including the closing of the north and south doorways to the church and their replacement with others in their present positions towards the west end of the church, giving access through the small lobbies to either side of the tower.

This building campaign, at the charge of the two parishes, is not well documented. The bills for the work have not been traced, but the following list of craftsmen was approved:

Thomas Piper, *mason*
John Harrison, *bricklayer*
Joseph Rhodes, *carpenter*
John Dowley, *smith*
John Poynder, *plumber*
Richard Gardner, *plasterer*
Mrs Everidge, *glazier*
Patrick Ross, *painter.*

The Rebuilding of the Roof and other changes: 1826–1827

In March 1826 James Savage reported that the party wall between the north wall of the church and the adjacent house known as 'No. 7 St Mary-at-Hill' was bulging, partly at least from water which had seeped into the wall. There is no record of what remedial work was done, but at some time it was rebuilt with separate walls to the two properties, presumably in the repairs of 1826–7. On 2 May 1826 Savage was formally appointed surveyor to the parish and later that year he drew attention to the decay of the roof timbering and recommended a complete replacement of the roof.[39] He also commented unfavourably that three of the main beams of the roof rested over window openings. As it had already been accepted that the leaded windows should be replaced with windows in iron frames, he recommended that the gothic windows then remaining should be replaced with others, round-headed and fewer in number, in less sensitive positions [*Figs R8 and R9*]. In carrying out this work Savage completely redesigned the roof, providing intersecting barrel vaults with a dome and lantern [Plate 6*a; Figs 8 and R12*]. His roof survived until the fire of 1988, and the replacement roof has the same appearance.

Earlier, in 1670–74, the east and the west walls of the church had been constructed with pilaster responds to the four columns. It was not possible to have these on the north and south walls as the late mediaeval windows occupied the positions [*Figs 3b and R5*]. With these mediaeval windows now blocked, matching pilasters could be provided [*Figs 3c, R8 and R9*].

It seems that the earlier blocking of the east window had made the chancel area very dark. To improve the level of lighting in this area, a new window, semicircular in shape, was opened in the pediment in a position over the altar piece [*Figs R10 and R11*].

Not all Savage's recommendations were accepted by the vestry, notably his proposal for a new burial vault below the floor. The vestry decided early in the campaign 'that at all events whether an entire new roof be adopted or not, the lantern in the present roof be not retained', suggesting that it was by then giving rise to trouble, probably by leaking rain water.[40] Despite this comment, the lantern may have been retained, clad in lead sheeting.

The total cost of the work done in 1826–7, some of which was not paid for until 1828, amounted to £5105. 3*s*. 4*d*., of which £120, being repairs to the vestry room, was met by the parish of St Mary-at-Hill alone, the remaining £4985. 3*s*. 4*d*. being divided between St Mary-at-Hill and St Andrew Hubbard.[41] This sum includes a payment of £244. 1*s*. 0*d*. to Savage for his services. The greater part of the work was undertaken by the same Thomas Piper, mason, acting as principal contractor, who had undertaken the earlier work under George Gwilt.

Some idea of the thoroughness of the refurbishing of the church can be gained from the details revealed in the bill of Best and Sons, drapers, of Greenwich, which included the following:

> A Communion Table Cloth of the richest Crimson Silk Velvet, bound all round with the best Gold Lace, one inch broad trimmed

---

Fig. 7 (opposite) *The west end of the church, as rebuilt by George Gwilt in 1787–8. (Drawing, The British Architectural Library, RIBA, London.)*

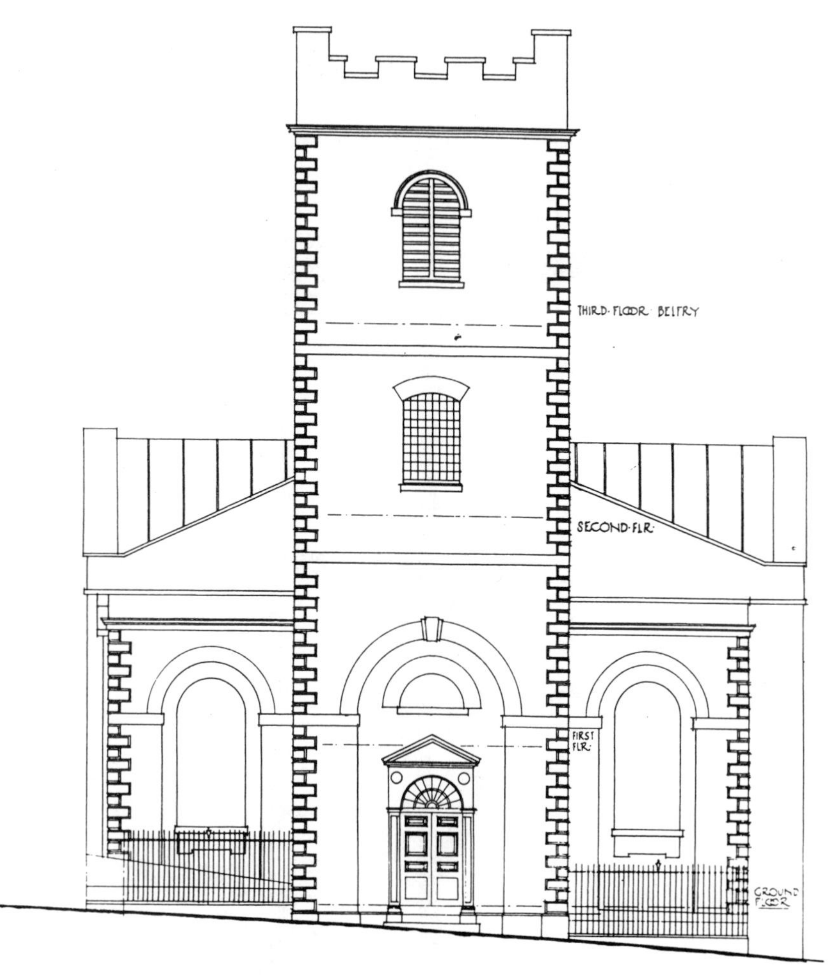

ELEVATION TO LOVE LANE

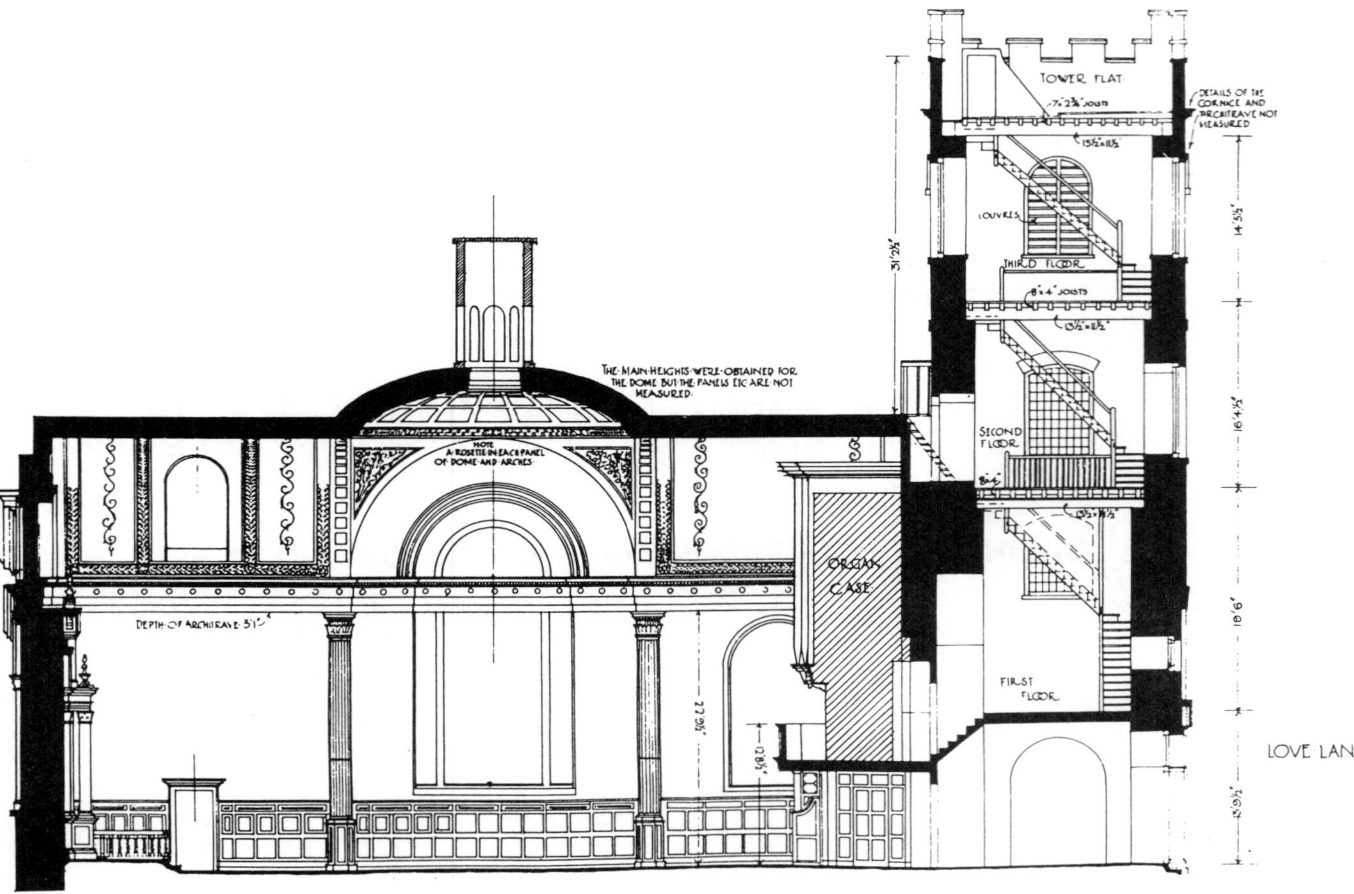

TOWER FLAT
DETAILS OF THE CORNICE AND ARCHITRAVE NOT MEASURED
LOUVRES
THIRD FLOOR
8"x4" JOISTS
SECOND FLOOR
FIRST FLOOR
ORGAN CASE
14'5½"
16'4½"
18'6"
13'9½"
31'2½"
27'9½"
12'8½"
THE MAIN HEIGHTS WERE OBTAINED FOR THE DOME BUT THE PANELS ETC ARE NOT MEASURED
NOTE A ROSETTE IN EACH PANEL OF DOME AND ARCHES
DEPTH OF ARCHITRAVE 3'1"
LOVE LANE

with rich ¾ inch Gold Fringe, ornamented round the bottom with 2¼ inch Gold Lace, the whole surmounted with a richly embroidered Gloria in Gold Pearl lined complete, £48. 5*s*. 9*d*.

2 Cushions for the Communion Table en suite, £4. 16*s*. 0*d*.

4 rich Gold Tassels for do., £34. 10*s*. 0*d*.

A rich Crimson Velvet Valance for the Pulpit do. with extra Gold Lace, £17. 19*s*. 3*d*.

A large Pulpit Cushion, en suite £5. 2*s*. 9*d*.

2 large rich Gold Tassels for do., £4. 15*s*. 0*d*.

A rich Valance for the Reading Desk, £10. 0*s*. 0*d*. etc. [42]

A Brussels carpet was provided for the chancel, a carpet for the pulpit stairs, crimson silk damask curtains for the organ gallery, curtains for the churchwardens' and other pews and 148 cushions for sixty-two pews.

Repairs and other Changes: 1848

In February 1848 the vestry appointed a committee 'to examine the state of the church to consider of the cleansing and repairs necessary and proper to be done',[43] again appointing James Savage to be surveyor. These repairs and redecoration, undertaken so soon after the repairs and reconstruction of 1827, may have been initiated as a result of a fire.[44] At that time the vestry had funds available from the sale of property in the St Katharine's area then being redeveloped. Savage's report deals mainly with cosmetic matters, with no major items of repair or replacement proposed. In a further report he suggested a number of improvements which could be made to the church and its fittings, including the blocking of the new semicircular window over the altar and the provision of two new roundheaded windows in the barrel vault (referred to as 'the eastern waggon head').

Fig. 8 (opposite) *The church in section, from the north, showing Gwilt's tower of 1787–8 and Savage's new windows and roof of 1826–7. (Drawing, The British Architectural Library, RIBA, London.)*

While this work was in progress he reported that the whole of the dome and some of the roof of the church was infected with dry rot and would need replacement.

The structural work was put in hand together with changes to the furniture and fittings in line with the ideas and concepts of the time, involving changes to the pews, pulpit, altar piece and other woodwork, much of which was undertaken with new carving in late seventeenth century style by William Gibbs Rogers. Most of this woodwork survives, although not currently returned to the church after the 1988 fire [Plates 7, 8, 10*b* and 15*a*].

The repairs and changes made to the lantern were not satisfactory. In November 1852 William Were, churchwarden of St Andrew Hubbard wrote to the St Mary-at-Hill vestry:

> I have requested Mr Piper to send some one to inspect the Lanthorn at the Top of the Church and to find out the cause of the wet entering the Church – last Sunday during Church time the dropping was at the rate of a Quart in the Two hours . . .[45]

He received a tart reply from St Mary's to the effect that the state of the lantern had not escaped notice and it would be attended to by the churchwardens of this [St Mary's] parish. James Savage having died earlier that year, the parish turned to Edward Fulkener, who responded:

> the evil is occasioned by the peculiar construction of the lantern, which consists of an inner and outer casing, the interval between which being not accessible, the rain penetrates to this division through the open louvres of the outer casing, and that to prevent the rain so entering it might be found necessary to change the form and construction of the lantern, which would be attended with considerable outlay and which I would submit is not necessary.
>
> I would therefore simply advise that one or two of the windows be taken out so as to get to the inside of the lantern, and that a larger lead gutter be fixed at the base of the lantern, with proper waste pipes.[46]

The work carried out to Fulkener's direction appears to have been satisfactory, as no further complaints are recorded.

In 1891 the church was closed on the plea that the structure was, in some unspecified way, unsafe and, in 1892, a faculty was obtained to enable the human remains interred within the church to be exhumed for re-internment at Norwood Cemetery. Some 3000 bodies were said to have been removed.[47] The church was reopened on 23 February 1894.

The War of 1939–1945; Repairs and Changes 1962–1968

The church of St Mary-at-Hill escaped destruction in the war of 1939–45, but suffered minor damage in the bombing of nearby property. Badly-needed repairs to the external stonework and stucco were undertaken in 1962 and the church closed again in 1967 for restoration by Seely and Paget. This involved extensive cleaning and repairs to the wood and plaster decorations. Some of the nineteenth century and earlier glass was resited, but much of the Victorian glass removed entirely. The electrical system of the church was rewired, Victorian chandeliers removed, and a new system of lighting with fluorescent and spot lamps introduced. New chandeliers were installed in 1968.[48]

The Fire of May 1988 and Restoration 1990–1992

On the night of Monday, 10 May 1988 the church was once again severely damaged by fire.[49] The flames were first spotted in the church tower by a watchman in a neighbouring building who called the fire brigade. It took eight hours to extinguish the fire and the damage was extensive. The dome had collapsed leaving much of the vaulting in a precarious state [Plate 12*b*]. The lantern was badly burned and the timbers were smashed when it crashed to the floor of the church destroying many of the pews beneath [Plate 13]. A considerable quantity of water had been used to extinguish the fire and this caused subsidence to the floor and damage to the furniture and fittings, including the pews, pulpit and organ. The masonry of the tower, although damaged by the heat of the fire, remained structurally sound, but much of its interior was gutted above first floor level. The roof and wall tops of the tower were left structurally unsound.

Despite the damage the only area of total loss was the roof built by Savage. Otherwise the early archaeology, mediaeval, seventeenth and eighteenth century work remained capable of repair, albeit with significant intervention for structural reasons. Consequently, options such as demolishing the church, or making alterations which would compromise the remaining fabric were limited. English Heritage, unable (because of ecclesiastical exemption from listed building control) to give formal advice, reported:

> In our view there is a strong case for advocating that the roof should be rebuilt as a replica of that which existed before the fire, i.e. to the design of James Savage. We take this view because we are concerned to maintain the integrity of the building as a historic structure, and because it . . . has implications for the work which will follow.[50]

However, the decision to repair the church was not immediately reached and rumours abounded that it was to be declared redundant and alternative uses sought for the site. Eventually, the view prevailed that, because of the enormous importance of the church, the amount of the remaining historic fabric and the fact that there had been insurance cover, it should be restored at an estimated cost of £1.5 million for the main work and a further £0.8 million for repair and replacement of the furniture and fittings. A faculty was obtained by architects The Conservation Practice (Project Architect John Barnes) and in 1990 the work was put in hand. The building contract was awarded to Ashby and Horner with the main specialist work being undertaken by Cowley Structural Timber Work Limited (structural timber work), TP Leadwork Limited (leadwork), Roger Bullivant (piling), Bingdon Builders (masonry), J Cooke and Sons

Limited (plaster work), A E Houghton and Son Limited (specialist joinery). The first phase of the work included:

> The demolition of damaged structures, the excavation of the floor and the provision of pile caps in consultation with archaeologists from the Museum of London; the installation of mini-piles and a concrete suspended floor; reconstruction of a new laminated timber dome with laminated cross beams and lead covering together with insulation and ventilation . . . various masonry repairs to the external structure and reconstruction of the wall heads . . . providing support and enclosure to the new roof.[51]

The Floor in the main body of the Church

Although the fire had blackened the walls of the church they remained structurally stable and required only minor repairs, but the water used in the fire fighting had undermined the floor. The presence of a large number of burial vaults and the likelihood of significant below ground archaeology meant that a simple compacted or ground bearing floor could not be put back without the cost and delay of extensive archaeological excavations. Instead, a scheme for a suspended floor utilising end-bearing minipiling was devised to leave the archaeology undisturbed. The contractor's programme had to await the investigation by the Museum of London to discover locations where the piling could occur. The structure was then adapted to suit the archaeology.

Each stone for the floor was recorded in position and numbered before it was lifted and then re-laid on the new floor structure exactly in the same place so that the layout of the heating ducts and box pews is repeated and the floor pattern maintained.

The Main Roof Structure

A survey of the roof was carried out, recording both Savage's roof and lantern [*Fig. R12*], neither having been adequately recorded prior to the fire.

Although it would have been desirable to replicate the Savage roof, the cost and timetable for erection were prohibitive, and it was decided that since all the material would be new, a new construction technique was acceptable so long as the form and appearance were true to the original [Plate 14*a*]. The glue laminated structure which forms the new roof has ribs and beams in the same location as the previous roof but with fewer timbers making up each element. Plywood has been used instead of butt boarding as the roof skin to complete the stability of the structure and to form the base for the lead. From start to finish the erection of the new roof took 13 weeks using a gang of four roofers.

The roof is a complex structure consisting of four barrel vaults forming the arms of the cross with a hemispherical dome at the intersection which is crowned with a lantern. Structural analysis showed that this design carried substantial lateral thrusts into the side walls. On three sides these thrusts are contained by massive walls and adjacent structures, but the east wall overlooking St Mary-at-Hill is thinner and has no such restraint. Therefore, it was necessary to include in the structural solution a tie system at the east end and to take down Wren's pediment to build in a steel beam.

The Leadwork

The leadwork on the main roof helps to outline the gentle external forms of the dome and the barrel vaults which can still be enjoyed from the buildings surrounding the church. In addition to the main roof, the porches and the tower roofs have been covered in lead sheet to match previous detailing. New guidelines and regulations required the discreet inclusion of ventilation and less spacing between rolls, but the specialist contractor has faithfully reproduced the pattern of the lead as recorded from the original roof.

The Plasterwork

The technology of fibrous plaster decorations has changed little since the original ceilings were created in the early nineteenth century. Flat areas were plastered in the normal way and the decorations cast in sections so that they could be fixed in place without lengthy or complex site operations. Modern rubber moulds meant that larger and multi-layered sections could be cast in one, although the materials and the skills remained the same. Fallen fragments were used to replicate the patterns, rosettes and mouldings of the new ceiling at the church, and site dimensions together with early photographs enabled an accurate reconstruction to take place [Plate 15*a*].

The Masonry

Extensive repairs were carried out to the stonework, brickwork and renders in order to repair damage caused by the fire and to provide much needed maintenance. An area of brickwork on the tower was so severely damaged by the heat of the fire and then the cooling of the water that the face had to be entirely rebuilt. The stones of the Wren east wall cornice fractured and became unstable so that each was provided with a new backing in order that the weight was kept back over the wall top. The opportunity was taken to remove areas of hard cement render, replacing it with softer lime stucco, and also to remove harmful pollution deposits.

The Joinery

Prior to the main contract the joinery was removed from the church and put into a store so that the moisture content of the wood could be stabilised and to avoid damage during the major works. While in store it was sorted and analysed in the anticipation that fund-raising will enable full restoration. The large west wall screens dated 1672 were repaired *in situ* so as to avoid disturbance of the ancient glazing, and a new oak staircase was constructed in the tower to match the one which was burned.

The Church Now and in the Future

In October 1991, a year after the first phase of the work had started, the roof was ready to receive the lantern and a grand Topping Out Ceremony took place presided over by The Right Honourable the Lord Mayor of London. On 12 December 1991 a carol service was held in the church by candlelight, which again was attended by the Lord Mayor, in order to celebrate its reopening as a place of worship.

It was intended that this first phase of the work would be followed by a second which would include the reinstatement of the oak pews, pulpit, reredos and gallery, a refurbishment of the organ and a return of the remaining fittings including the sword rests, royal coats of arms etc. The cost of this phase was not covered by the insurance and a separate fund raising exercise was envisaged. However, so that the church could function once again the wainscot panelling was repaired and refitted, the gaps in the floor slab where the pews will be were filled to form a level base, the bare masonry where the reredos should be was hidden behind a large curtain, and the exposed structure of the west gallery was temporarily carcassed in new timber.

At the time of writing the building is in full use as a parish and ward church, but its future is being considered by the Bishop of London in the wider aspect of the future use of churches in the City Deanery following the report produced by Lord Templeman.[52] In anticipation that the building will continue in use as a City church, an initiative by the Friends of City Churches is raising funds for the reinstatement of the furniture and fittings. A grant has been sought from the National Heritage Memorial Fund.

THE DECORATION OF THE CHURCH

AN unpainted strip still exists across one of the western pilasters, suggesting that in 1674 the church was brought into use with bare walls. This bare state may not have lasted very long, the first decoration of the building being recorded on 3 May 1685 when the vestry reached agreement with Henry Doogood that he should whitewash the church. On 9 August there were bills for 'whitewashing, painting and repairing'.

Even before the building had been completed the churchwardens were turning their attention to the provision of furniture and fittings for it. On 14 May 1672 it was agreed to borrow £500 or £600 at interest for the finishing of the church pews and other things (unspecified) and to buy and hang two bells. The cost apparently exceeded the expected sum and in order to get the vestry of St Andrew Hubbard to pay a further amount, the vestry of St Mary-at-Hill ordered, on 27 January 1680, that an account be drawn up of the 'cost and charges of the pewes, pulpitt, font, and Communion table'. [53]

No provision is recorded for a clerk and reader's desk, wainscoting or altar piece. Of these, a desk is referred to on

15 February 1685 when (with the pulpit) it was to be hung in mourning. No record has been found of when the wainscot was initially installed. The lower parts of the walls had been left by the masons in a rough stage and it is reasonable to assume that wainscot would have been a priority as soon as the fabric of the building had been completed. Its removal after the fire of 1988 revealed a change to the bases of the pilasters on the east wall which must date from soon after the completion of the building, possibly associated with the wainscoting. The surface of the east wall behind the altar was in poor condition, much of the surface having been removed to resite the altar piece. It is impossible to tell if this area had originally been painted, but the existence of some areas with a chocolate-coloured paint suggest that it was soon done.

The omission of any reference to an altar piece or reredos in the list of fittings is perhaps more significant. It may be assumed, from the paint on the wall behind the reredos, that in the early years after the construction of the church, there was no altar piece in place. The earliest reference to one is in 1708, when it was described by Hatton [*see the entry under 'Reredos', page 45*], but the description does not tally with the reredos known to us [Plate 10*a*], being somewhat smaller. The tablets with the Creed, Paternoster and Decalogue, would have been installed soon after the completion of the building (although there is no reference to them in the vestry minutes), and the most likely arrangement is for them to have been mounted directly on the east wall. Such an arrangement is believed to have existed at St Mary-le-Bow from its completion (at about the same time as St Mary-at-Hill) until 1706. No doubt the parishioners and vestrymen were aware of the elaborate altar pieces then being installed in other churches, but there is no reference in the vestry minutes to any action being taken by the vestry to provide one for St Mary-at-Hill; it may have been installed in 1706 when Andrew Snape was appointed rector.

Hatton described not only the reredos but also the decoration of the east wall.[54] The 'window with pilasters' had not then been obscured by the reredos, and above it was a Glory 'whose rays issue out of an equilateral triangle gilt with gold'. It is unlikely to have been carved in stone or moulded in plaster, and was probably just painted on the wall, soon after the time when the reredos was provided.

Later decoration of this east wall, as recorded by Malcolm, indicates that it had paintings of the Virgin Mary and St Andrew in positions on either side of the reredos, above the Paternoster and Creed, described as 'but tolerable', which were framed by curtains painted on the wall.[55] Such curtains, painted in crimson on the east wall are known from other churches, notably St Stephen Walbrook.[56]

THE 'BECKFORD' SWORD STAND

FURNISHINGS AND FITTINGS

described in alphabetical order

ALTAR and Sanctuary. In accordance with the practice of the time the church was rebuilt, the sanctuary was placed against the east wall of the church, occupying the centre bay. Its position was marked by a small raised platform, probably like other churches of the time, no more than one step in height, and paved. No special paving material was named, and it may simply have been in Purbeck stone. It was later paved with black and white marble to a chequered pattern, renewed in 1881 [Plate 10*a*].

The altar or communion table is said to be of Wren's time. It has five legs carved and twisted at the top, curved stretchers and moulded and enriched top. The altar rails have carved and twisted balusters and flat carved standards, quadrant-shaped angles and carved top rail. They, too, are probably of the late seventeenth century.

In the seventeenth century the sanctuary was separated from the body of the church only by the altar rails and there is no record, in the fitting out of the church, of any elaborately carved sanctuary screen such as that provided at St Peter, Cornhill and at All Hallowsthe-Great. However, in a table of burial fees dated 1714 there is reference to the dues payable for burial below the north and south doors to the screen, suggesting that a sanctuary screen of some kind had by then been installed.[57] In 1854, in a letter to the bishop, mention is made of oak carving which had been added to the chancel screen in 1849.[58] A photograph by Latham taken before 1896 shows no such screen suggesting that it had by then been removed, probably in 1881 or when the church was closed in 1892–4.[59]

Bells. Prior to the Great Fire of 1666 there were six bells in the church, all of which were destroyed in the fire. By 1672 the tower had been sufficiently repaired to take bells once more and the churchwardens were instructed to borrow money at interest for, amongst other things, the purchase and hanging of two new bells. Repairs of 1753 included a new stock for the Great Bell and a rehanging of both. In 1788 the parish asked Messrs Mears of Whitechapel to provide three new bells with frames for the church. The largest was to be twelve hundredweight, the second nine hundredweight and the third seven hundredweight. The company was to allow the parish for the metal of the old bells, indicating that they were replacements rather than additions to the complement of bells. The bells have still to be returned to the church after the fire of 1988, although provision for them to hang was made in the reconstruction.

Cistern. The first supply of water to the church was probably rain water collected from the roof into a cistern. Such a system may have existed from late mediaeval times, but the earliest record of a cistern is not until 1756 when it was in position at the western end of the church. It was presumably fed by a down pipe from a rainwater head. The present lead cistern is in the churchyard on the north side of the church [Plate 11*b*]; it is dated 1788. It is trapezoidal, suggesting that it was made for a corner where the walls were not entirely square, possibly in Lovat Lane where the tower seems to have been aligned to the lane rather than the church. It is decorated with embossed bands of a wave design incorporating leaves. It has a vase of flowers between two panels with the initials St M. H. and St A. H. respectively and figures representing a sower and a reaper. Such designs of cistern were common in the London of the eighteenth century, although most of them have now disappeared.

Clocks. Expenditure on the various clocks is hard to disentangle from the accounts. A 'Dyall and Watch' were to be put in hand in 1678/9 and in 1695 payment was made for the repair of damage to the clock case incurred when the church was being repaired. In 1699 a Mr Clements was paid £2. 5*s*. 0*d* for cleaning and mending the 'parish Clock and Watch'. A new 'dyall' for it was erected in 1705. There are occasional references to repairs to the clock, but none to any purchase. The restoration of 1826–7 included work by Sharp and Sons for the repair and cleaning of the turret clock with a repairing and gilding of both dials. This was apparently a striking clock then in the tower. There was a separate clock in the organ loft whose 18 inch dial was cleaned and repaired at the same time. The remains of three clocks have recently been identified in the great vault.

Doorcases. There is little information now available concerning the earlier doorcases on the north and south sides of the church. These were likely to have been in oak and to have been installed as part of the original fittings soon after the building was finished in 1674. There is a record that the church had a lion and unicorn as part of the carved oak south doorcase, but this may have come from some other furnishing, possibly the reredos. Its present whereabouts is unknown and it must be presumed lost; it cannot be the present lion and unicorn, discussed below.

Font and font cover. The font was provided at the expense of the parishioners soon after 1672. It is described by Allen[60] as 'large and handsome . . . of marble, of an octagonal form, more modern than the [Great] fire' [Plate 11*a*]. He noted that it was then at the west end of the south aisle. Fonts are more moveable than many other items and its position may have changed several times. However its present position is close to that of the old mediaeval and Wren period south doorway, conceivably the most important entrance to the church. The description shows it to have an 'octagonal white marble bowl with reeded enrichment, baluster-stem with acanthus enrichment, black marble base' and the font cover as 'carved oak . . . with cherub-heads and swags, ogee-shaped upper part with enriched angles and terminal'.[61]

Galleries. There is no evidence that St Mary-at-Hill ever possessed galleries on the north and south sides of the building. The first gallery to be constructed was at the west end of the church in front of the tower, to accommodate an organ purchased by public subscription. A bishop's licence was given on 3 March 1692/3 for a gallery with 15 feet frontage and 18 feet depth, which was presumably erected in 1693. The central section of the existing gallery (from joints revealed in the woodwork in 1991) probably marks this original small gallery, 'plain' and not then bow-fronted.

On 12 September 1722 the vestry ordered that a gallery should be made 'adjoyning on each side the Organ gallery for the Convenience of the Charity Children to sit in'. Alterations to it were discussed in 1764, when an estimate was sought for bringing the organ case forward. It is however by no means certain that any work was done at this time. In 1787 Gwilt proposed supporting the gallery by iron pillars. As the sections of the gallery to either side of the central portion are now supported with these, it can be assumed that this was done. From these extensions, further wings stretch to the north and south walls of the church. These were probably installed in 1849 [Plate 8; *Fig. 9*].

CROSS SECTION

LOOKING TOWARDS GALLERY FRONT

Lectern. A lectern was presented to the parish by the rector, the Revd Arthur Trower, on 23 March 1876.

Lion and Unicorn. Elizabeth and Wayland Young commented that the lion and the unicorn have the initials VR on their breasts.[62] It therefore seems likely that they are the work of William Gibbs Rogers dating from 1848–9 and would not have been part of the reredos. They may have been intended as embellishments to the pew used by the Lord Mayor, acting as supporters to a sword stand.

Organ. In late mediaeval times the church possessed two organs, listed in an inventory of 1553 as one larger than the other.[63] There is also a reference in the vestry minutes to 'the little organs in the choir'. Payments are recorded to both William Mundys and Thomas Tallis, indicating a high standard of musical life in the parish at that time.

The church as rebuilt after the Great Fire was without an organ until 1693 when the gallery was built for it and a subscription list opened. A total of £330. 5*s*. 6*d*. was collected. It was probably provided by Father Smith, but few details of it were recorded. He is named as providing additional stops in 1708. An undated specification, recorded in a document formerly in the church[64] was published in 1943–4.[65]

By 1764 this organ was much out of repair. Estimates were obtained but it is doubtful if much was done as it was replaced in 1787–8 by a new instrument by Samuel Green at a cost of £320 plus the old organ. This was again replaced by a new organ in 1848 to the design of William Hill in a case described as 'in seventeenth century style'. In 1880 Messrs Hill and Sons added a choir organ and

---

Fig. 9 (opposite) *The church in section from the east, showing the west gallery and organ. The gallery, whose centre is of 1693, was extended probably in 1849. (Drawing, The British Architectural Library, RIBA, London.)*

bourdons, both placed outside the case, in the south part of the gallery [Plate 8]. This organ suffered damage, probably as a result of an unrecorded fire in the tower and was completely overhauled and rebuilt in 1971 by Messrs Hill, Norman and Beard, with most but not all of it in the original case which apparently survives from the seventeenth century. It now awaits further cleaning and overhaul after the fire of 1988.

The first record of any choir seems to be in 1856 when the rector, Arthur Trower, obtained approval from the vestry for a payment of £40 per year to the organist for paying singers. By 1881 the choir consisted of 19 voices.

Pews and West Screen. The church was re-pewed after the restoration of 1670–4. Further pews were added from time to time (as in 1714, when four new pews were placed in the cross aisle), partly perhaps to give increased seating accommodation, but also no doubt to increase the revenue from pew rents. The vestry minutes make frequent reference to repairs to the pews, including the need to rehang the doors.

On 30 June 1684 the vestry ordered that the two upper pews in the north and south aisles should be made for the accommodation of the best women in the parish. In 1722 a Mr Serocole, an inhabitant of the parish of St Andrew Hubbard, was given permission to have a pew on the north side of the Communion Table for his family, he to decorate both it and the corresponding pew on the south side of the church with carved work. These pews were removed in 1881 together with those at the east end of the north and south sides of the church.[66] Choir seats were provided from the recovered material.

Pulpit and Tester. A new pulpit was made in 1503–4. It was of wood, fixed to one of the pillars of the church and approached by ladder. It was destroyed in the Great Fire of 1666.

Plate 1 The pre-Fire church and its surroundings, from the south. In this detail from Hollar's print of 1666, St Mary-at-Hill church is number 37. (Print, Guildhall Library, Corporation of London).

Plate 2(a) The same view as Plate 1, after the Great Fire. (Print, Guildhall Library, Corporation of London).

Plate 2(b) The pre-Fire church, enlarged from Hollar's 'Long View' of 1647. (Print, Guildhall Library, Corporation of London).

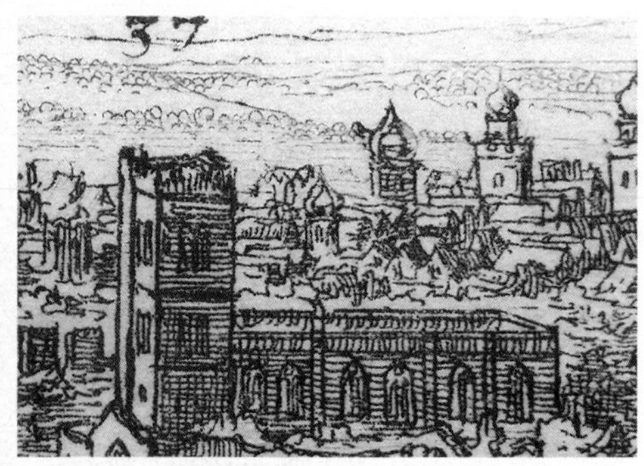

Plate 2(c) The church after the Fire, a detail from Plate 2(a). (Print, Guildhall Library, Corporation of London).

Plate 3 The church at the turn of the century, looking south down the street called St Mary-at-Hill, showing Wren's east end with its subsequent alterations. (Photograph, RCHME Crown Copyright).

Plate 4 The exterior in the early years of this century, looking down Lovat Lane from the north, showing Gwilt's west end and tower. (Photograph, RCHME Crown Copyright).

Plate 5 The interior in about 1896, looking north-east. (Photograph, G.H. Birch, *London Churches of the XVII and XVIII Centuries*, 1896).

Plate 6(a) The interior, looking south-east, showing the barrel vaulted roof and decorative plaster work. (Photograph, RCHME Crown Copyright).

Plate 6(b) Capital of a column, photographed after the fire of 1988. Compare with *Fig. 4*. (Photograph, English Heritage).

Plate 7 The interior, probably in the 1920s, looking north-west, showing the arrangement of the box pews. The hanging sheet was used as a projection screen. (Photograph, Guildhall Library, Corporation of London).

Plate 8 The interior, probably in the 1920s, looking south-west, showing the finely carved west gallery and organ. The sword stands appear to have been temporarily removed. (Photograph, RCHME Crown Copyright).

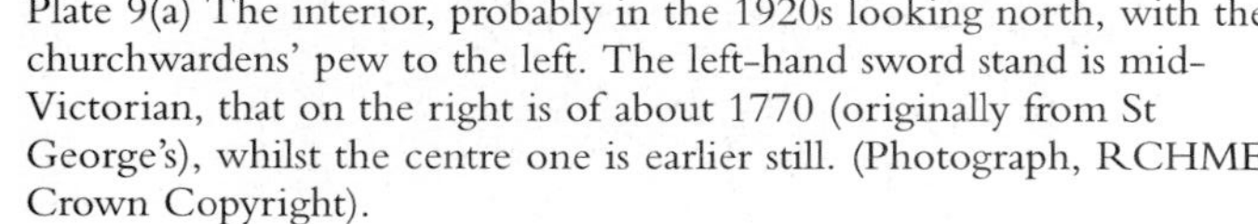

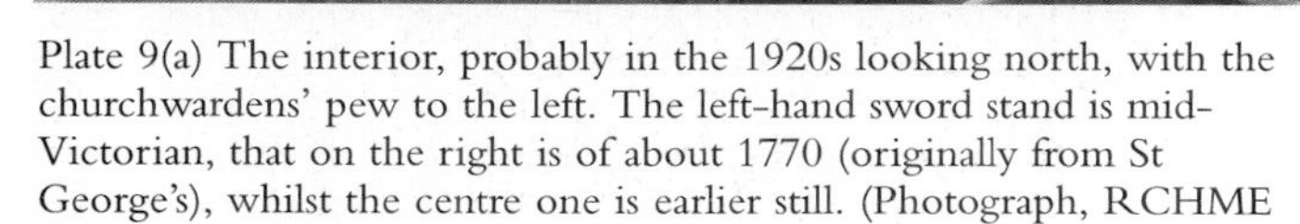

Plate 9(a) The interior, probably in the 1920s looking north, with the churchwardens' pew to the left. The left-hand sword stand is mid-Victorian, that on the right is of about 1770 (originally from St George's), whilst the centre one is earlier still. (Photograph, RCHME Crown Copyright).

Plate 9(b) Two of the sword stands in the 1880s. On the left is the 'Beckford' stand of about 1770, on the right the somewhat later 'Sainsbury' stand. (Photograph, Guildhall Library, Corporation of London).

Plate 10(a) The reredos in the early years of this century. (Photograph, Guildhall Library, Corporation of London).

Plate 10(b) The pulpit, earlier this century. (Photograph, Guildhall Library, Corporation of London).

Plate 11(a) The font. (Photograph, RCHME Crown Copyright).

Plate 11(b) The eighteenth century cistern, dated 1788, and with the initials of St Mary-at-Hill (St M.H.) and St Andrew Hubbard (St A.H.). (Photograph, RCHME Crown Copyright).

Plate 12(a) The Resurrection panel. It probably date from about 1600. (Photograph, RCHME Crown Copyright).

Plate 12(b) The roof, shortly after the fire of 1988, looking west. (Photograph, *The Independent*/Geraint Lewis).

Plate 13 Interior, shortly after the fire of 1988, looking east. (Photograph, RCHME Crown Copyright).

Plate 14(a) The new roof under construction. (Photograph, English Heritage).

Plate 14(b) The new roof after completion. (Photograph, The Conservation Practice).

Plate 15(a) The interior, showing renewed plasterwork. (Photograph, The Conservation Practice).

Plate 15(b) Shephard's print of about 1831, here enlarged, after bricking up of the east window. The window in the pediment has since been blocked – compare Plate 3. (Print, *London and its Environs*, (1829-31), Guildhall Library, Corporation of London).

Plate 16(a) Gwilt's tower and west front (1787-8), shown in a print of 1814. Note the square-headed windows in the south wall, remaining from the pre-Fire church, and replaced by Savage in 1826-7. (Print, Guildhall Library, Corporation of London).

Plate 16(b) The roof before replacement by Savage's roof in 1826-7. (Print, Guildhall Library, Corporation of London).

In January 1788 it was ordered that the pulpit should be placed against one of the pillars at the east end of the church, and that the reading desk should be against another. Discussion concerning the pulpit continued and in September the vestry ordered that a sounding board should be placed over the pulpit. It is not certain that this was done as by November there was a request 'to wait on the Proprietor of the New Meeting [house] in Grub Street to inform him they have a Pulpit, Reading Desk and Clerk's Desk with Chandiliers and Irons to dispose of'. There is no record of any receipt indicating a sale, nor of any subsequent replacements, suggesting second thoughts by the vestrymen.

In 1848 the vestry appointed a sub-committee to approve a design for the pulpit. This may have been no more than an enrichment of the old pulpit, with the addition of new carving by William Gibbs Rogers [Plate 10*b*].

Reredos. At St Mary-at-Hill, the reredos is set hard against the east wall of the church [Plate 10*a*]. Certain of the architectural features of the wall have been chiselled away to take it and some of the framing elements are set within the plaster surface of the wall. It was described by Hatton in 1708 as:

of Norway Oak, with a Cornish and Cartouche pediment, whereon is placed the Queen's Arms, and, at some distance, the Supporters. The Commandments are done in black on Gold, under a Seraphim, between two Cherubims; and there are other Enrichments of Cartouches, Fruit &c and above all, near the Roof, are the Paternoster and Creed; but so high, that they are not easily legible.

Malcolm's description of the reredos was given in 1807:

This is of the Composite order, and consists of four isolated pillars, with entablatures, urns and seven candlesticks on them, and a beautiful attic with a circular pediment; two pilasters for intercolumniations for the tablets of the Creed and Paternoster; and the centre contains those of the Decalogue, over which is a nimbus, the word Jehovah and Cherubim, and in the tympan carvings.

There is also a slightly later description by Allen:

The altar is composed of carved oak of the Corinthian order, and is decorated with four fluted pillars, sustaining an entablature and attic, on the cornice of which are seen golden candlesticks and the royal arms, besides a variety of carving.

This description dates from 1828 and relates to the church with the changes introduced by Savage. Both the later descriptions recall the present reredos in the way that Hatton's does not, but neither has sufficient detail to confirm that it refers to the altar piece exactly as it now exists. The plasterwork and gilding that is now apparent behind the reredos is clearly associated with Savage's remodelling. It suggests that, following his restoration, the part of the wall with gilding that is now hidden was then exposed to view. Since the reredos would have stood as close to the east wall as possible, it may be assumed that the altar piece was not then as tall as it is now. This would be consistent with both Malcolm's and Allen's descriptions. Further changes were made to the east end by Savage in 1848. The reredos was 'to have the gilding cleansed from the vases and carved ornaments. The candles removed and flowers and flames added to match the other ornaments and the whole restored . . . the gilding of the tablets and mouldings round as at present.'[67] The attic story of the reredos may have been added at this time, the additional height hiding some of Savage's gilding of 1828.

Royal Coats of Arms. The church possesses two Royal Coats of Arms, both undifferentiated Stuart. Those which were, until the recent fire, in the centre of the gallery front were probably made for the church and at one time a part of the reredos [Plate 8]. The other came from St George, Botolph Lane.

Sword stands. From the latter part of the sixteenth century it was customary for the Lord Mayor to attend in State one or other of the City Churches in his term of office.[68] The attendance was usually, although not always, in the Lord Mayor's own parish church, and generally in the ward of which he was an alderman. He was accompanied by the sheriffs and common councilmen of the ward and escorted by the sword-bearer and mace-bearer, the former carrying the State sword and wearing the Cap of Maintenance. These formal state visits of the Lord Mayor were discontinued in 1883, in the mayoralty of Robert Fowler.

For these visits a stand was required on which the sword could be placed during the service. These stands are generally referred to as sword stands but also as sword rests or sword cases, and occasionally as sword irons, although some of the earliest were made of wood. They are now mostly of wrought iron and decorated with painted coats of arms. The number of these arms varies, some irons having as many as five or six which would probably include the Royal Coat of Arms, the City Arms, the Arms of the Livery Company to which the Lord Mayor belonged, and his or her own personal Coat of Arms. St Mary-at-Hill has four sword stands of its own to which were added two from St George, Botolph Lane, to give one of the best collections in the City [Plates 9*a* and 9*b*]. Together they span a period of over two hundred years and in that time became increasingly more complex and decorative.

Wainscot. Following the reconstruction of the church in 1670–74 the church was wainscoted throughout and much of this has survived. However, frequent changes within the church have required alteration, notably in the centres of both north and south sides where the old doorways were removed, in the north-east corner where the wall was rebuilt, in the south east corner where the position of the vestry door was changed, and in both north and south sides in response to the provision of heating in the church. There has thus been both a reworking of old material and the provision of new. The wainscot was damaged in the 1988 fire, but has now been repaired and replaced.

PROJECTING CLOCK, AT EAST FRONT OF CHURCH

HEATING AND LIGHTING

THE first record of any heating in the church was in December 1765 when the vestry ordered that two iron braziers be provided 'in order to air and warm the church in damp and cold weather'. These were presumably open, coal-burning stoves and probably far from efficient in heating the church, although they lasted until 1788. In that year the vestry again discussed the heating of the church and decided to replace the stoves with new ones with the proprietary name of 'Buzaglo'. However, on 2 September 1788, instructions were given to purchase 'Register' rather than 'Buzaglo' stoves, which the vestry decided 'would answer the purpose better'. They too were placed within the church itself. Chimneys on both north and south sides of the building suggest that the stoves were placed approximately in the centre of these walls, but a second opening to a flue on the south side, revealed behind the wainscot in 1991, indicates that at one time there were two coal burning stoves along this wall.

In his report on the church James Savage noted that:

At present the two fires draw the air necessary for their own combustion from the body of the Church whence it passes rapidly up the flue with the smoke – the air thus drawn from the body of the Church is supplied by fresh cold air entering at the casual openings in the building and a great deal has come in from the illformed lead lights . . .[69]

On his recommendation the two existing stoves were replaced by a warm air stove with new flues, at a cost of £150. They were installed in 1828, apparently in a vault under the south side of the church, as a vestry minute ordered that the 'shed over the stairs to the furnace vault be covered with slate'. They were not satisfactory and by May 1833 the flues and 'cockles' of the stoves had to be replaced. In 1835 it was reported that 'the present hot air dispenser being found so defective and dangerous . . . it was resolved that the church be warmed by means of a hot water apparatus'. The pipes for this were at first above the floor level but, in 1848, on the recommendation of James Savage, they were placed below.

Church services were held in daylight – evensong being held in the afternoon – and when illumination was required it was candlelight. The earliest accounts refer to tallow candles, hanging candlesticks, candlestick bowls and sconces. For more general illumination 'branches' or branched candlesticks were used. These were of iron or brass and to be found in different parts of the church. What was referred to as the large branch was given to the parish by Thomas Lenhall, a Deputy of the Ward, in 1678. In 1719 it was proposed to dispose of it, replacing it with three smaller branches, each of which was to carry an inscription recording the original gift. A new chandelier was bought on 15 April 1789.

The first introduction of gas lighting seems to have been in September 1811 when a gas light lamp was ordered to be erected in the church passage. The Gas Light Office was to charge three guineas per annum, engaging to 'cleanse, light and extinguish the same'. In

July 1826 the vestry resolved that the church itself should then be lighted with gas:

> resolved 16 lights in the Body and Gallery and that there be one or more lights in the Ante Church. Each light including glasses with ground glass globes similar to those in the Parish Church of St Lawrence Jewry.[70]

Gas was to be supplied at a cost of fifteen shillings per thousand cubic feet. One of the lights was placed on the pulpit, but this was subsequently removed and wax candles substituted in 1846. One can well understand that the harsh gas light would prove to be a distraction to all those bent upon listening to the sermon.

Electric lighting was first installed in 1892–4 while the church was closed for repairs.[71]

THE 'SAINSBURY' SWORD STAND

THE BURIAL OF THE DEAD

Churchyards

IN spite of references to the *great, little, green, pardon* and *procession churchyards*, there is no evidence that there were ever any more than two. Both were in use as cemeteries until the mid-seventeenth century, but after the Great Fire that to the south fell into disuse and subsequently disappeared. The north churchyard remained in use, although gradually reducing in size. Constant burial in it had so increased the level of the ground that in 1750 the vestry ordered the soil, to an extent not exceeding two hundred loads, to be taken away.

The north churchyard was closed for burials by order of the vestry dated 21 May 1846. A tablet recording this was placed on the north wall of the church. In July of that year the parish purchased a plot of ground, 72 feet by 63 feet, from the South Metropolitan Cemetery Company, Norwood, for the sum of £567. The churchyard, now paved at a level above that of the floor of the church, remains as an open space, with access from St Mary-at-Hill.

Burials within the church

Burials within the church have taken place for most of the 800 years that there has been a church on the site. Some of these were in brick-lined graves intended for one, four, six or more bodies. The human remains from within the body of the church, amounting to some 3000 bodies, were removed in 1892–4, and these bricklined graves were probably destroyed at the time. Few of these were recorded, and none were found in the recent excavations. In 1815 the vestry recommended that no more brick graves should be allowed within the church.

The church also had a number of vaulted graves of brick construction, paid for by the more affluent citizens of the parish and intended for family burials. In 1826 the vestry ordered that a search be made for the vaults and a plan of them prepared. If this was done, the plan has not survived. With the exception of the larger vaults for multiple burials, the vaults known to remain are all ranged along the east wall of the church. Like the simpler graves in the body of the church, they were emptied in 1892–4.

The vault in the northernmost bay of the east wall may have been that of a certain John Woods. A memorial to the Woods family now on the adjacent north wall of the church indicates that its members were buried beneath. The son died in 1670 and the vault was presumably constructed soon after, possibly the first to be built in the new church. On the south wall of the church at its east end is a monument to one John Harvey, who died 1700, indicating that he was buried in an ancestral vault 'near this place', which could be the vault on the south east corner.

The earliest of the larger vaults, intended for multiple burials, is that constructed by Joshua Marshall in 1670–2. It is on the south side of the church with dimensions given as 18 ft in length, 9 ft in width and 7 ft in depth. This is the vault referred to in the seventeenth century as the Great Vault.

A rector's vault was constructed for Edward Lake, rector 1682–1704, possibly in 1684 when bills for it were audited. It was probably in the south east corner of the church, although not within the chancel area. Further vaults have been located on the north side of this rector's vault, including one within the chancel area. This would have been for one of the rectors, possibly John Brand, who died in 1806 and was buried in the chancel. A new large vault was constructed c.1715, known at the time as the New Great Vault, but subsequently simply as the Great Vault. This was in the centre aisle, occupying most of it. The entrance was from a position below the tower. This vault served for most of the burials within the church, although some were elsewhere within the building.

Following public concern of dangers to health arising from the practice of burying bodies inside churches, an Order in Council was issued on 10 February 1859, closing the vault. Instructions were given that the coffins within should be laid on the floor, covered with 1½ feet of earth and this covered with 6 inches of powdered charcoal. The entrance steps were to be bricked up and a ventilation shaft from the vault extended as high as the roof of the church. The vault was later opened and cleared of coffins and human remains.

In 1758 a pit to house human remains from the churchyard was dug to a depth of fourteen feet beneath the floor of the great vault. All knowledge of the existence of this repository had probably been forgotten by 1892 and it is unlikely that it would have been cleared of human remains at that time.

Monuments

Cobb refers to four hatchments for George IV, Queen Adelaide, Duchess of Kent (mother of Queen Victoria) and the Prince Consort.[72] They are no longer on display and their present whereabouts are unknown. It was the practice to provide such hatchments during periods of mourning and examples are known from other City churches.

The monuments within the church are not necessarily in their original positions. Some of those now on display were brought from the neighbouring church of St George, Botolph Lane, destroyed in

1901. Those existing in the church in 1826 were taken down and replaced by Savage in what was described as 'a more uniform manner'. None of them can be said to be of the highest quality.

Resurrection panel

The resurrection panel [Plate 12*a*], carved from a single stone block now fixed to the north wall of the north lobby, was reported to have been at one time over the entrance to the church passage at the Lovat Lane end. The subject of the panel, a resurrection scene, suggests that it may originally have been located over a gate to one of the parish churchyards. Similar panels are known from other London churches, including St Giles-in-the-Fields and are believed to date from about 1600.

THE RESURRECTION PANEL

BILLINGSGATE WARD AND ITS PARISHES

ALL of the churches belonging to the six parishes in Billingsgate Ward were destroyed in the fire of 1666 [Plate 2*a*; *Fig. 2*]. In the reorganisation which followed, only three were rebuilt, St Mary-at-Hill serving its own parish and that of St Andrew Hubbard; St George, Botolph Lane serving also St Botolph, Billingsgate; and St Margaret Pattens serving also St Gabriel Fenchurch.

The continual decline in the population of all these parishes made some scheme for the amalgamation of these parishes inevitable.[73] In 1901 the united parishes of St George, Botolph Lane with St Botolph, Billingsgate were, by Order in Council, further united with those of St Mary-at-Hill and St Andrew Hubbard.[74] The church of St George, Botolph Lane was then demolished and the site sold.

In 1954, under a scheme for the rearrangement of pastoral supervision, the care of the united parishes of St Margaret Pattens with St Gabriel Fenchurch passed to the United Benefice based upon St Mary-at-Hill, with the church of St Margaret Pattens then converted to a guild church.[75]

There is thus now only one parish church in the ward of Billingsgate, St Mary-at-Hill, established in 1953 as the Official Church of the Ward.[76]

AN EARLY SWORD STAND

NOTES AND REFERENCES

Abbreviations

The following abbreviations are used in the references:

BL	*British Library.*
GL	*Guildhall Library, City of London.*
K. Top.	*King's Topographical Collection, British Library.*
LAMAS	*London and Middlesex Archaeological Society.*
RCHME	*Royal Commission on the Historical Monuments of England.*

1. Henry Andrade Harben, *A Dictionary of London*, (1918), p. 394.
2. Richard Newcourt, *Repertorium Ecclesiasticum Parochiale Londinense*, (1708), p. 263.
3. BL Harleian MS 391; Derek Gadd, *LAMAS Trans.*,(1983), 34, pp. 171–77.
4. A. and G. Trower, *The Parish of St Mary-at-Hill, its Church, Estates and Charities*, (1878), p. 2.
5. Charles Lethbridge Kingsford, *Stow's Survey of London*, (1908), p. 105.
6. Paul Jeffery, Richard Lea and Bruce Watson, *LAMAS Trans.*, (1992), 43, pp. 192–200. See also Appendix A, where the archaeological investigations are summarised.

7. *The Mediaeval Records of a London Church (St Mary-at-Hill) AD 1420–1559*, Transcribed and edited by Henry Littlehayes, Early English Text Society, (1905).
8. GL, W. Hollar's 'Long View', (1647), and 'A True and Exact Prospect...', (1666).
9. Richard Lea, *Architectural Recording at St Mary-at-Hill Church*, February, 1985, Museum of London; *Popular Archaeology*, December 1985 / January 1986, pp. 22–4.
10. W. Hollar, *op. cit.*
11. Including St Anne and St Agnes, St Magnus-the-Martyr and also St Bartholomew-by-the-Exchange whose western stair turret was retained in the rebuilding after the Fire and demolished with the church in 1841.
12. Charles Clarke, *Architectura Ecclesiastica Londini*, (1820).
13. GL St Mary-at-Hill vestry minutes 1609–1752, MS1240/1, 21 July 1668.
14. GL Commissioners' Orders, MS 25540, p. 28.
15. 22 Charles II (1670), cap. 11.
16. Bodleian Library, Tanner 142/38, 23 March 1667.
17. A drawing of a street front elevation for St Edmund the King (All Souls' WREN II.44) is marked 'with his Maj[es]ties Approbation'.
18. GL MS 25540, p. 3.
19. City of London Record Office MS 222.11.
20. Christopher Wren, jr., *Parentalia*, (1750), p. 309.
21. *London Topographical Society*, The Survey of Building Sites in the City of London after the Great Fire of 1666, (1967), I, p. xvii.
22. GL Commissioners' Book of Contracts, MS 25542/1.
23. GL Building Accounts, MS 25539/2.
24. GL Commissioners' Book of Contracts, MS 25542/1 p. 71.
Further details of this sketch plan will be found below (page 61).
25. Edward Hatton, *A New View of London*, (1708), II, pp. 373–6.
26. GL Prints & Maps, Crace, E.2.1., No.111; Paul Jeffery, *London Topographical Record*, (1995), XXVII, pp. 119–134.
27. Robert Seymour, *A Survey of the Cities of London &c.,*(1734), I, p. 435.
28. G. H. Birch, *London Churches of the 18th and 19th Centuries*, (1896), p. 37.
29. Elizabeth and Wayland Young, *Old London Churches*, (1956), p. 109.
30. James Peller Malcolm, *Londinium Redivivum*, (1807), IV, pp. 415–425,
31. Nikolaus Pevsner, *The Buildings of England, London*, I, (1973), p. 169.
32. Mark Rogers, *Down Thames Street*, (1921), p. 133.
33. RCHME, *London IV, The City*, 1929, p. 17.
34. GL MS 25539/2.

35. GL MS 25539/6 and /8. None of the work seems to be of a major character, although the turret to the tower was rebuilt.
36. GL MS 25539/8.
37. GL MS 1240/2, 16 June 1767.
38. *Ibid.*, 8 May 1787.
39. GL MS 1240/3, 2 March 1826; 23 May 1826.
40. *Ibid.*, 13 June 1826.
41. GL MS 3886.
42. GL MS 10716.
43. GL MS 1240/4, 1 February 1848.
44. Howard Colvin, *A Biographical Dictionary of British Architects*, 1600–1840, (1978), p. 720.
45. GL MS 1240/4, 19 November 1852.
46. *Ibid.*, 3 November 1853.
47. Alfred Ernest Daniell, *London City Churches*, 2nd. ed. (1907), p. 240; Sir Walter Besant, *Survey of the City of London*, (1910), p. 270; Faculty, GL MS 18319/34, 1892.
48. GL Faculty, MS 21545/51.
49. *The Times*, 11 May 1988; *The Architects' Journal*, 1 June 1988; *Country Life*, 16 June 1988.
50. English Heritage, London Division, 3709, 22 November 1988.
51. *Ibid.*, 16 April 1991.
52. Lord Templeman, City Churches Commission, Diocese of London, Report to the Bishop, January 1994.
53. GL MS 1240/1, 27 January 1680.
54. Edward Hatton, *op. cit.*
55. James Peller Malcolm, *op. cit.*
56. As shown in a drawing by A. W. Pugin and Thomas Rowlandson in Rudolph Ackerman, *Microcosm of London*,(1808).
57. GL MS 23933.
58. GL MS 1240/4, 23 Februay 1854.
59. G. H. Birch, *op. cit.*
60. Thomas Allen, *The History and Antiquities of London*, (1828), III, p. 114.
61. RCHME, *op. cit.*
62. Elizabeth and Wayland Young, *op. cit.*
63. Henry Littlehayes, *op. cit.*
64. GL MS 23932.
65. R. Sinden Gilbert, *The Organ*, (1943–4), XXIII, pp. 118–122.
66. GL Faculty, MS 18319/4.
67. GL MS 1240/4, 14 March 1848.

68. E. H. Freshfield, *Archaeologia*, (1894), 2nd. ser. IV, p. 41.
69. GL MS 1240/3, 23 May 1826.
70. *Ibid.*, 10 July 1826.
71. Alfred Ernest Daniell, *op. cit.*
72. Gerald Cobb, *London City Churches*, revised by Nicholas Redman, 1989, p. 162.
73. GL MS 18463. In these miscellaneous papers, which relate to the union of St Mary-at-Hill with St George, Botolph Lane, the following figures for the population of the four parishes in 1871, 1881, 1891 are given:

PARISH	*POPULATION*		
	1871	*1881*	*1891*
St George, Botolph Lane	162	96	168
St Botolph, Billingsgate	154	99	-
St Mary-at-Hill	477	206	173
St Andrew Hubbard	139	89	-
TOTAL	*932*	*490*	*341*

74. *London Gazette*, 1 October 1901.
75. *Ibid.*, 2 February 1954.
76. *Ibid.*, 20 January 1954.

The Drawing of the Roof in the Book of Contracts (see note 24 above)

The Book of Contracts contains a pencil sketch (not a measured drawing) showing the roof structure in plan. It is about half a quarto page in size. Each timber is shown by parallel ruled pencil lines. In all but one case the timbers are drawn continuously – that is, where timbers cross each other or join each other no joint or break is shown (the one exception is not likely to be of any significance). The sketch is shown in stylised form overleaf.

The contract is dated 3 December 1670. The roof is to be 'of good Oaken Timber, according to a design and Model Brought in.' The scantlings are then given:

Wall Plates	11 : 9	Beames of *a*	9 : 11
12 Posts	13 : 13	Principalls of *a*	9 : 9
Beames of *B*	12 : 13	Beames of *b*	9 : 9
Principalls of *B*	12 : 10	Principalls of *b*	9 : 9
Beames of *A*	11 : 13	Rafters	5 : 2½
Principalls of *A*	11 : 10	Purloines	9 : 8
		Ceiling Joysts	5 : 2½

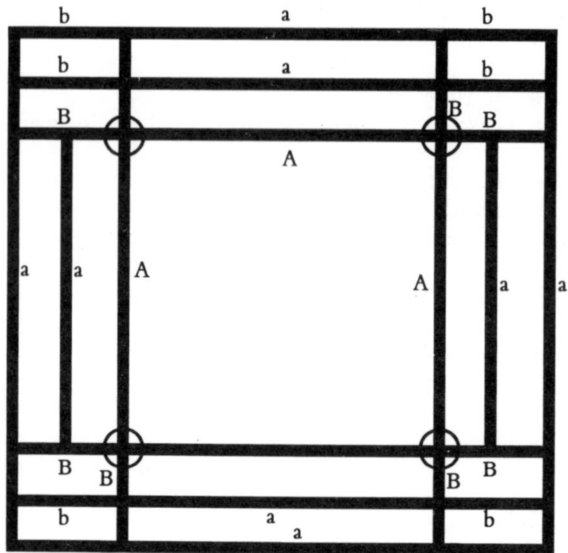

Further contractual details follow:

'The eight Trusses that beare the Cornice to be measured in upon one side of the Trusses, and for the Roofe thus framed & boarded with good deale without sap fit for the plumber the said Mr Lock shall receive £7. 00. 00.

'For the Ceiling Joysts upon the Flatt (except those that are between the four Pillars under the Lanthorne [)] at twenty shillings.'

APPENDICES

THE 'SYDNEY' SWORD STAND

Appendix A

AN ARCHAEOLOGICAL SUMMARY

Bruce Watson

Museum of London Archaeological Service

Introduction

FOLLOWING the damage caused to the church by the 1988 fire, a programme of archaeological work was carried out during 1989–91 by Museum of London archaeological staff as part of the restoration programme.[1] Only limited areas of the interior were examined, in advance of the drilling of a series of mini-piles and the digging of a network of shallow ground beam trenches to support the new floor. The excavations established that within some areas of the church the digging of numerous post-mediaeval graves and their exhumation during 1892–4 had caused considerable disturbance of archaeological deposits.

The Church before the Thirteenth Century

The church of St Mary-at-Hill is listed by John Stow the sixteenth century historian as one of five parish churches within the

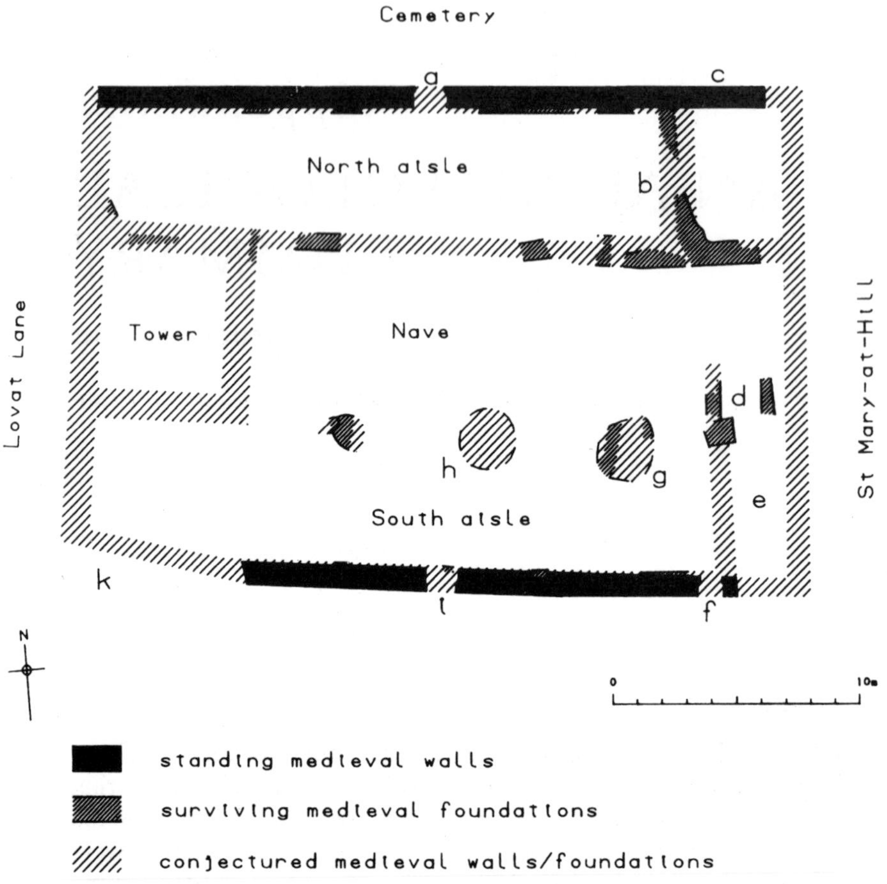

Fig. 10 *Evidence for the plan of the mediaeval church.*

a. *north door* b. *possible remains of north transept or east wall of pre-1487 north aisle* c. *rebuilt portion of north aisle* d. *burial vault* e. *burial vault* f. *door* g. *possible south transept* h. *postulated portion of pier base* i. *south door* k. *site of the Abbot of Waltham's Inn kitchen and possible cemetery*

Billingsgate ward.[2] The parochial link with the important Anglo-Saxon quay at Billingsgate and the fairly central position of the church within the ward suggests that it may have been the earliest church within the unit [*Fig. 2*]. If this interpretation is correct it would suggest that the church is of tenth or eleventh century date.

The only evidence for the existence of the postulated Anglo-Saxon or documented Norman church are four incomplete truncated supine Christian burials which were discovered under the foundations of the south arcade. These graves cannot be precisely dated but their depth suggests that they were probably part of an extra-mural cemetery, perhaps associated with an unlocated pre-thirteenth century church. A small church could have been situated on the site of the large eighteenth century vault under the western part of the nave. It was quite common for urban churches to expand in several directions from a small original building and to encroach on the surrounding burial ground.

The Mediaeval Church

Excavations within the present church have revealed extensive evidence of its mediaeval precursor, consisting of truncated rubble-built wall foundations found below existing floor level. Unfortunately, due to post mediaeval activity, there were no associated deposits to date these foundations, but on stylistic grounds they are probably of the 13th–15th century. As only small areas of the interior were investigated the complete plan of the mediaeval church was not recorded, but enough fragments were located to allow it to be conjectured [*Fig. 10*].

The mediaeval church had a west tower on the site of the present structure. There was a rectangular nave bounded on the north side by a continuous wall line, with a slight change of alignment at the east end which may mark the position of the choir or chancel. The south side of the nave was marked by three oval blocks of masonry interpreted as pier bases for arcading. It is possible that the south aisle was extended westwards along the south side of the tower in about

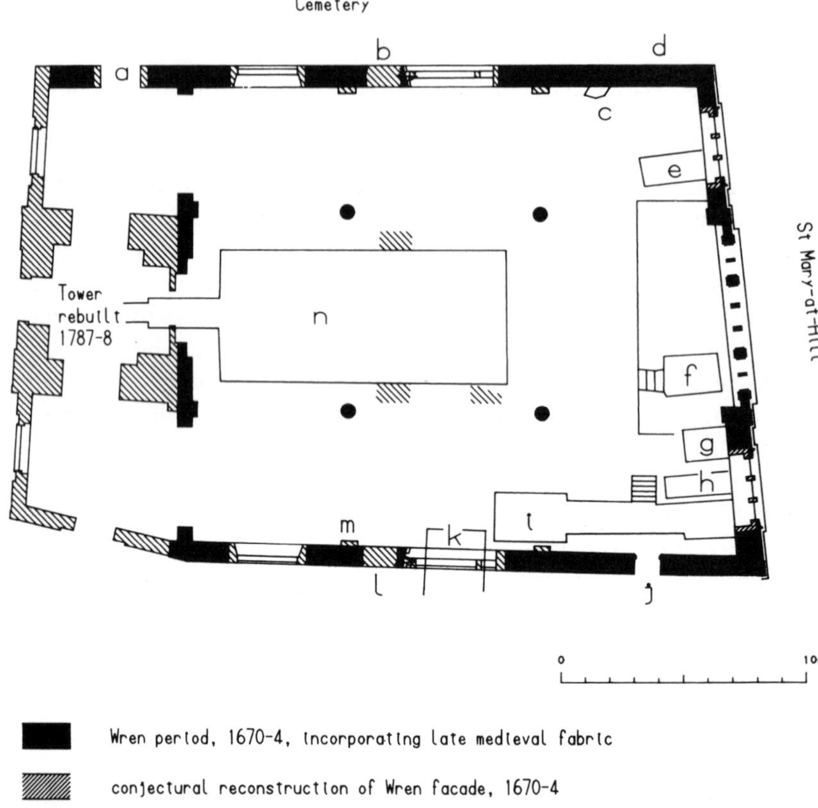

Fig. 11 *Plan of the Wren church, with later changes*

a. *north door added 1787–8* b. *mediaeval door blocked 1787* c. *cut back monument* d. *16th–17th century rebuild of eastern end of north wall* e. *17th century burial vault* f. *burial vault below altar* g. *burial vault* h. *burial vault* i. *three-chambered burial vault* j. *door to vestry* k. *19th-century boiler house* l. *mediaeval door blocked* m. *one of the four 1820s responds* n. *burial vault* circa *1715*

1500 or 1501.[3] The south arcade of the chancel was represented by a single rectangular pier base, with fragments of mediaeval burial vaults lying to the north and south of it. Some of the walls of the south aisle vault may have stood above ground level, possibly forming part of a south transept or St Katherine's chapel. Interestingly, both the north and south limits of the mediaeval nave were precisely followed by the two pairs of seventeenth century columns which now divide the nave from its twin aisles.

The first phase of the north aisle dates from about 1487,[4] and appears to have been rebuilt, or more likely extended eastwards, between about 1504 and 1666. A foundation extending northwards from the chancel marks either the east wall of the first phase of the north aisle or part of an earlier transept, possibly the site of St Stephen's chapel. The line of the mediaeval east wall of the church is uncertain due to realignment during the seventeenth century.

The Post-mediaeval Church

Below-ground archaeological work has little to contribute to the post mediaeval history of the church. During the excavations a series of seventeenth to eighteenth century brick-built burial vaults and the nineteenth century boiler house were located [*Fig. 11*]. In 1859 the large burial vault under the nave was sealed and during 1892–4 each vault was emptied and all post-mediaeval burials exhumed. All the vaults except for the large nave vault were then backfilled with soil.[5]

NOTES

1. Paul Jeffery, Richard Lea and Bruce Watson, 'The Architectural History of the Church of St Mary at Hill, in the City of London'. *LAMAS Trans.*, (1992), 43, pp. 192–200. Bruce Watson, 'Excavations and Watching Brief Observations (1989–91) at the Church of St Mary-at-Hill, Lovat Lane', (SMY88). *Museum of London Archive Report*, (1992).
2. H. B. Wheatley (ed), *The Survey of London by John Stow*, (1956), p. 435.
3. Discussed above, page 7.
4. Discussed above, page 6.
5. Sir Walter Besant, *Survey of the City of London*, (1910), p. 270.

Sideboard Recess for Doles

Appendix B
RECONSTRUCTION DRAWINGS

Richard Lea

Historical Analysis and Research Team, English Heritage

THE medieval and later masonry was exposed by the removal of wainscot panelling and repairs to the exterior, and it was recorded during 1991. Recording concentrated on those features which were to be concealed again behind panelling, paint, render or plaster.

The reconstruction drawings on the following pages are a selection taken from an unpublished detailed analysis of the historical development of the fabric of the church.

The drawings show the development of the church in four phases: the sixteenth century church, Wren's rebuilding after the Great Fire, Savage's rebuilding of the early nineteenth century, and the recent church.

THE 'BECKFORD' SWORD STAND FROM ST GEORGE'S

LIST OF RECONSTRUCTION DRAWINGS

In the drawings, recorded fabric is shown in *black*, reconstructed elements are shown in *red*.

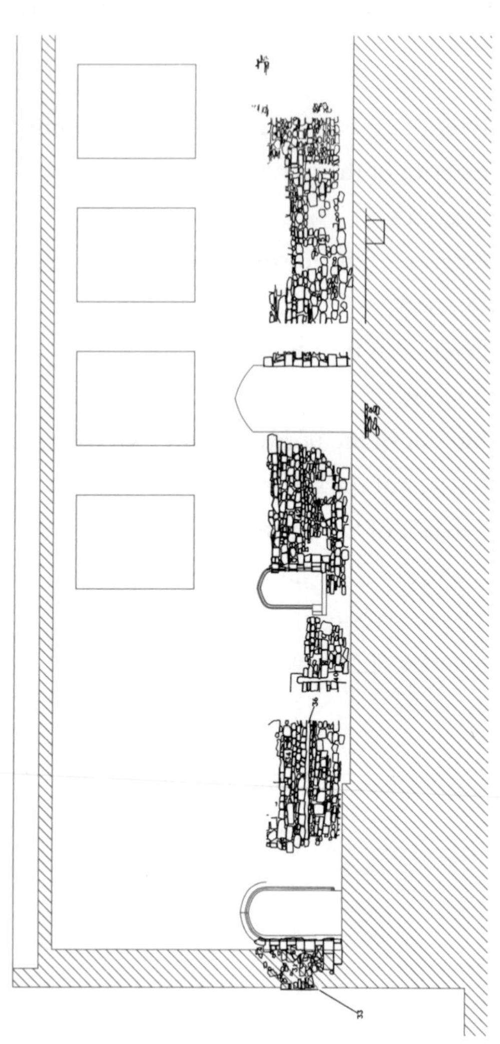

Fig. R1 *Interior of the south wall in the sixteenth century*

The interior of the south wall in the sixteenth century, showing windows, central entrance doorway, probable vestry door and cupboard or piscina. (*See page* 7.)

Three openings were exposed in the south wall of the church. The largest matched that in the north wall and, although blocked with later masonry, was recognisable as a door from the quoins forming the west jamb. At the east end of the wall, next to the cut back return for the east wall, was a double-ogee moulded jamb with a chamfer stop and the springing probably for a four centred head. Again the actual opening was blocked by later masonry. The mouldings clearly suggest a door opening southwards through the wall and hence a vestry attached to the church. The third opening, between the two doors, was apparently for a piscina or cupboard. The surviving west jamb was moulded with a double ogee between two fillets. Plaster was not removed from the upper parts of the wall. The reconstructed windows are based on the rectangular windows shown in the Coney and Skelton view of 1814 [Plate 16a].

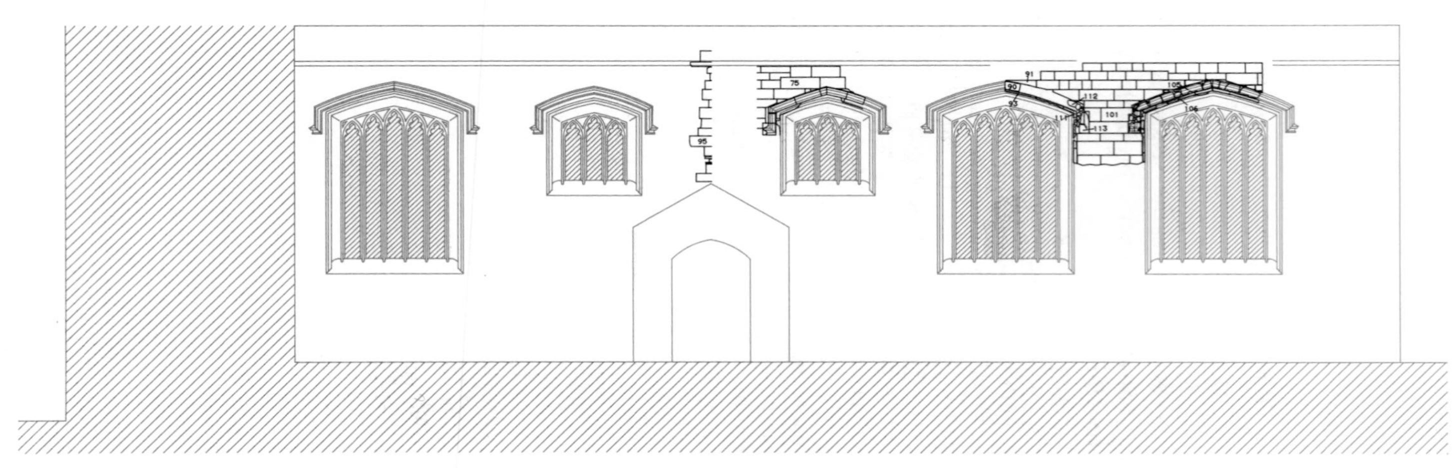

95
75
91
90
93
112
111
101
113
105
106

Fig. R2 Exterior of the north wall in the sixteenth century

The exterior of the north wall in the sixteenth century, showing the form and position of windows and the central north door. (*See page* 7.)

The two windows at the west end of the wall had already been recorded in 1984, by the Museum of London (Museum of London Archive Report, Site Code MAH 84). The removal of render during the repairs of 1988–91 exposed parts of three pointed segmental windows set in a ragstone ashlar wall face. All three were blocked and the hood-moulds cut back flush with the wall face. The reconstruction of the east window was based on observations on the pattern of later rendering which repeated the sequences observed for the western three. The jambs for the door were observed on the opposite side of the wall. The reconstruction of the second window from the window above the door is based on symmetry; all traces would have been removed by the construction of the present large north window. Evidence for the tracery patterns probably survives within the thickness of the walls but during the repair programme there was no need to investigate these areas. The moulding pattern shown in the reconstruction is a combination of roll and hollow chamfer commonly found in late fifteenth and sixteenth century City architecture.

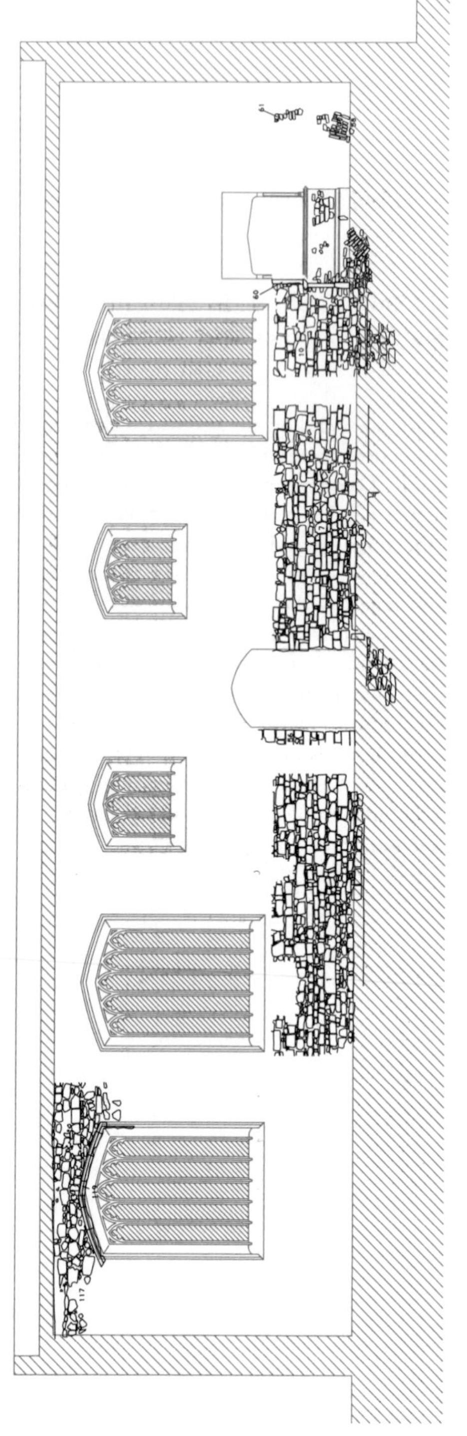

Fig. R3 Interior of the north wall in the sixteenth century

The interior of the north wall in the sixteenth century, showing the windows, the central north door, and a possible Easter sepulchre.

The head of the west window was recorded in 1984 by the Museum of London. The windows are reconstructed on the basis of the evidence recorded on the north side of the wall. The door was blocked with later masonry but the quoins of the jamb were clearly discernible in the ragstone rubble facing of the wall. The absence of mouldings on the internal wall is consistent with the siting of the door on the outer face of the wall. At the east end, fragments of moulded Purbeck or Petworth marble set in the wall face were broken off flush with the wall face. The style of the mouldings and their location approximately on the line of the altar step indicate a tomb of the Easter Sepulchre type described by Bridget Cherry in 'Some New Types of Late Medieval Tombs in the London Area', British Archaeological Association, Vol X, (1990).

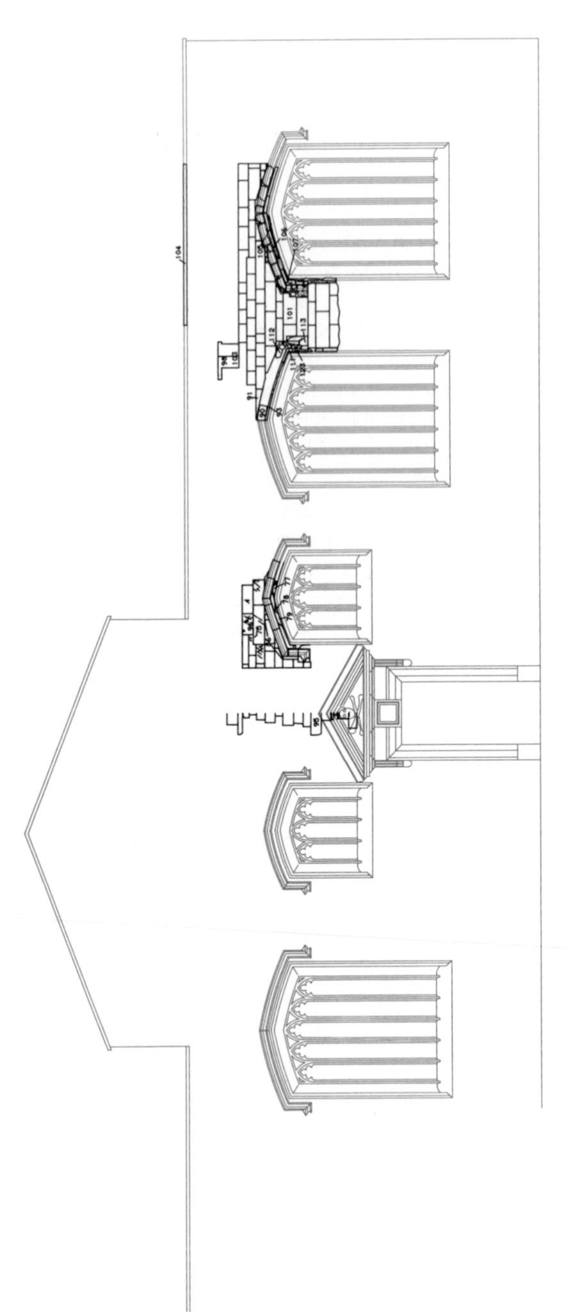

Fig. R4 The exterior of the north wall after Wren's rebuilding (1670–1674)

Whereas the east wall was completely rebuilt by Wren, the tower, north and south walls survived the Fire, including the arrangement of the windows, which survived until the nineteenth century. The drawing, of the exterior of the north wall, shows how little was changed. (*See pages 14–15.*)

The north door acquired the death's head doorcase now located at the east end of the passage south of the church. A gable must have been added to accommodate the transepts in the ceiling shown in the Guildhall Crace Collection drawing [Plate 16*b*].

117
118
52
53
55
1
56
7
10
60
61
59
12
13
14

Fig. R5 *The interior of the north wall after Wren's rebuilding (1670–1674)*

Examination of the interior of the north wall after the 1988 fire revealed a surprising juxtaposition of Wren's classically defined interior space and the medieval fenestration. The responds on the north wall were not added until the nineteenth century (*see page 24*). The roof was clearly conceived with little regard for the medieval bay system. Nor was the north door central to the transept expressed in the roof. The four columns at the centre of the church, and the pilasters at each end of the nave without corresponding pilasters on the side walls, would, to some extent, have continued the effect of the medieval arcade.

127
138
124
124

Fig. R6. *The exterior of the east end after Wren's rebuilding (1670–1674)*

The east wall above ground level was wholly rebuilt by Wren (*see pages 15–16*). The facade has since been altered in ways which significantly alter our perception of the underlying architectural form, although much of the original detailing survives *in situ*. The original Venetian window was blocked following the installation of the reredos in 1767 (*see page 21*). The mullions and transoms were left *in situ* but those in the side windows were probably removed at a later date.

Traces of the transoms for the side windows survive in the coursing of the jambs and in returns in the bead moulding. The semi-circular mullion in the centre window is based on the returns in the bead moulding on the transom and the absence of similar features in the soffit of the surrounding arch. This form of tracery, which can be paralleled in other Wren buildings such as St Bride's and the Sheldonian Theatre, Oxford, is Dutch in character. The broken pediment was slightly damaged when the present 'D' shaped window was inserted in the nineteenth century but the original return in the cornice survived largely intact. This insertion removed all the traces of the original treatment of the centre of the pediment. The oculus shown in the reconstruction, presumably blind or ventilating the roof void, is therefore very conjectural. The location of the carving above the side windows was suggested by the break in the pattern of coursing. The larger blocks were roughly finished which suggests that they were cut back *in situ* flush with the wall face. The swag under the centre window was suggested by the documentary reference to festoons totalling 57 feet in length (*see page 15*). The panel under the centre window was not stripped during the repairs but is the most likely location for the additional footage.

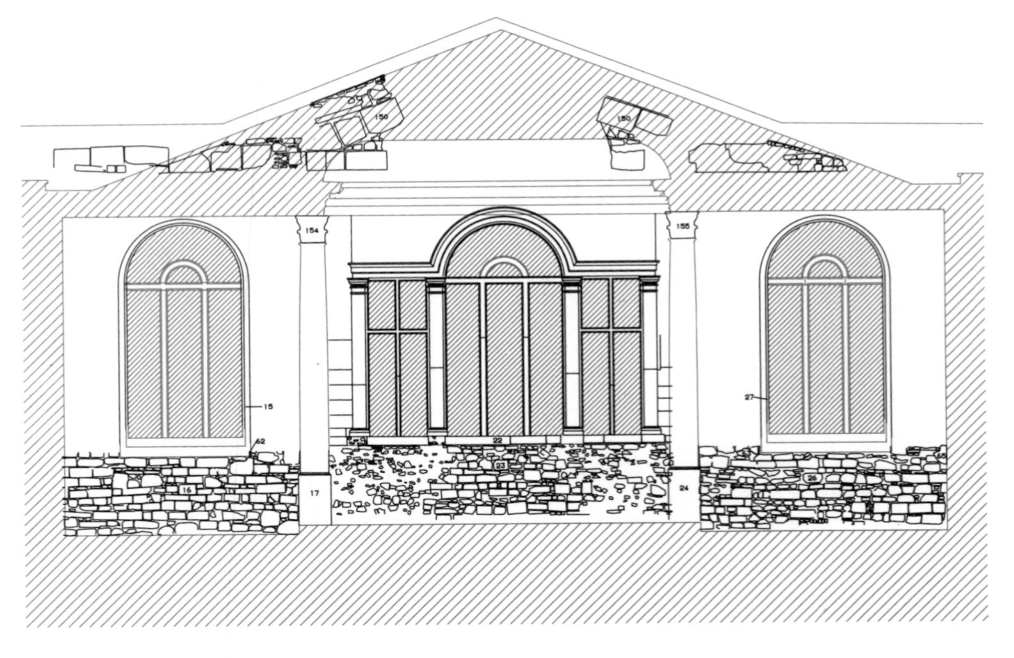

150
150
154
155
15
62
16
17
22
23
24
27
26

Fig. R7 The interior of the east end after Wren's rebuilding (1670–1674)

The removal of the panelling and reredos after the 1988 fire allowed a reappraisal of Wren's interior. At the east end the large expanses of glazing would have provided a great deal of light.

The pilasters between the choir and side aisles were plain, not fluted, and matched those at the west end of the church. The capitals in the Venetian window, related in design to the composite capitals used for the central four columns, bore traces of gold leaf. The coved ceiling and roof line shown in the reconstruction are taken from the cross section through the building in the Crace Collection [Plate 16*b*].

117
102
54
5
52
53
55
1
4
3
56
57
74
6
8
7
159
9
60
10
12
13
61
59
14
58

Fig. R8 The interior of the north wall after Savage's rebuilding (1824–5)

Savage re-ordered the north wall interior elevation, adding pilasters to match the central four columns, and inserting large round headed windows (*see page 23*). The north door had already been moved to the west end by Gwilt in 1787–8 (*see pages 21–22*).

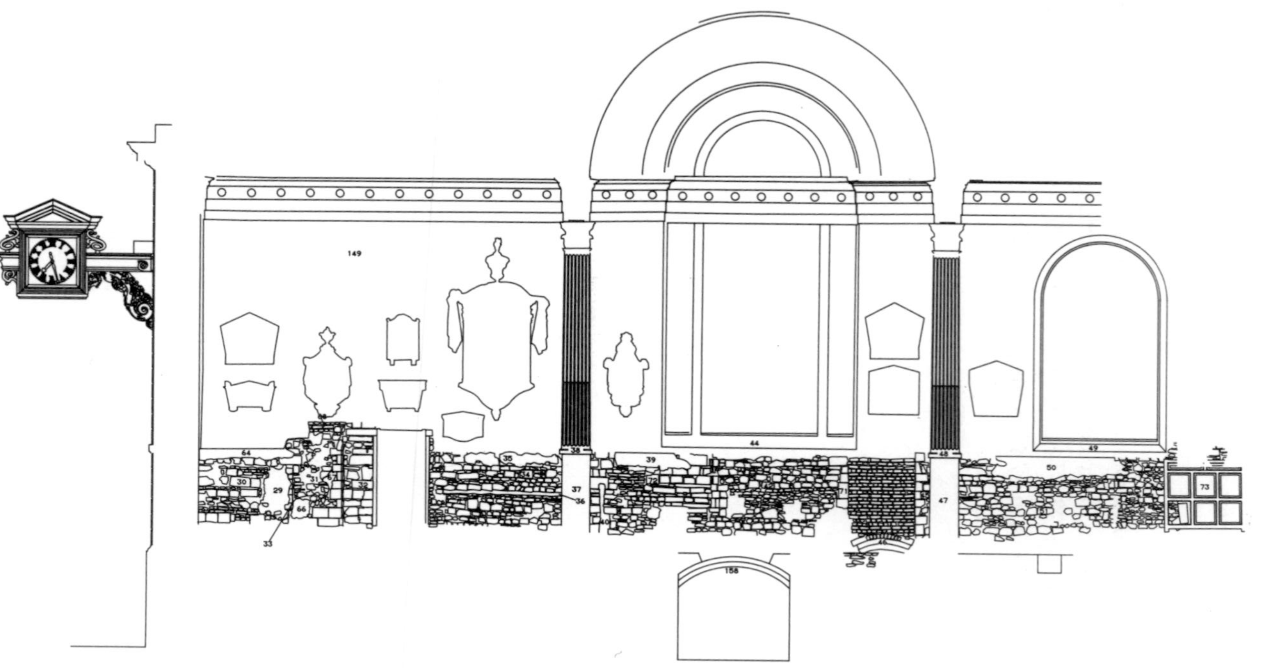

160

Fig. R9 The interior of the south wall after Savage's rebuilding (1826–7)

The south wall was treated in much the same way by Savage as the north. As in the north, the south door had already been moved by Gwilt (*see pages 21–22*).

The bracket clock appears in views of the church from the early nineteenth century. It is, however, of a type more commonly found on the west front or tower of City churches from the early eighteenth century. It is possible that it was originally set in the tower at the west end of the church, the more typical location for clocks of this kind. If so, its relocation probably followed the rebuilding of the tower by Gwilt. Until the second half of this century it was driven from the tower by a complex arrangement of axles.

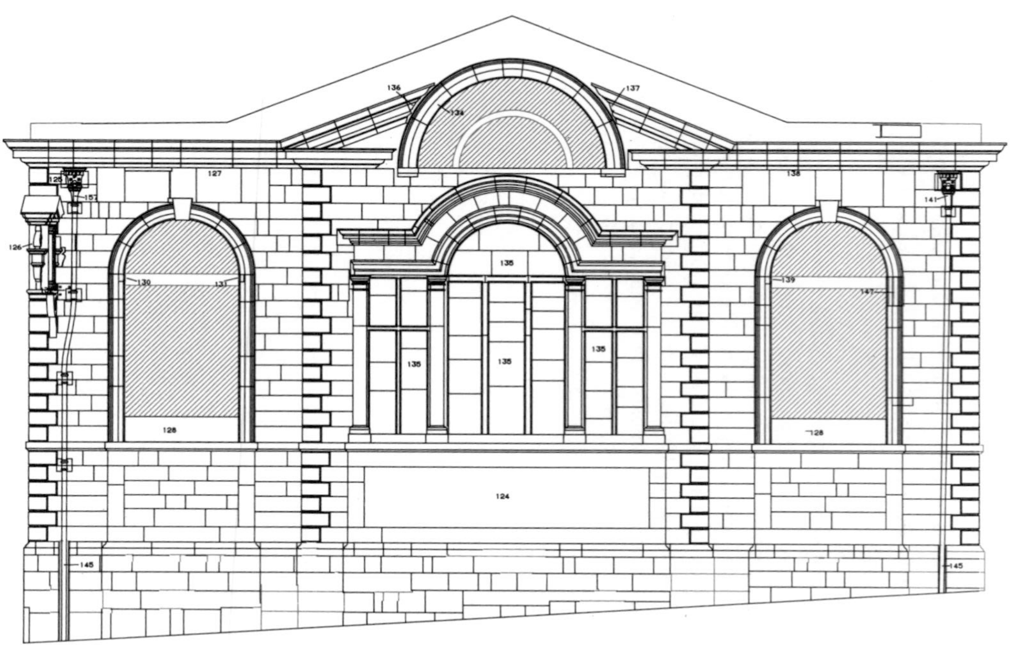

136
134
137
127
138
125
151
141
126
130
131
135
139
147
128
124
145

Fig. R10 The exterior of the east end after Savage's rebuilding (1826–7)

The exterior of the east end had already been transformed by the blocking of the east window. Savage inserted the 'D' shaped window in the pediment and removed Wren's tracery from the side aisle windows and fitted them with deep transoms. (*See page 24.*)

This arrangement was recorded in the view by Godwin and Britton in 1839 [*Fig. 6*]. The festoons or swags had by then been removed.

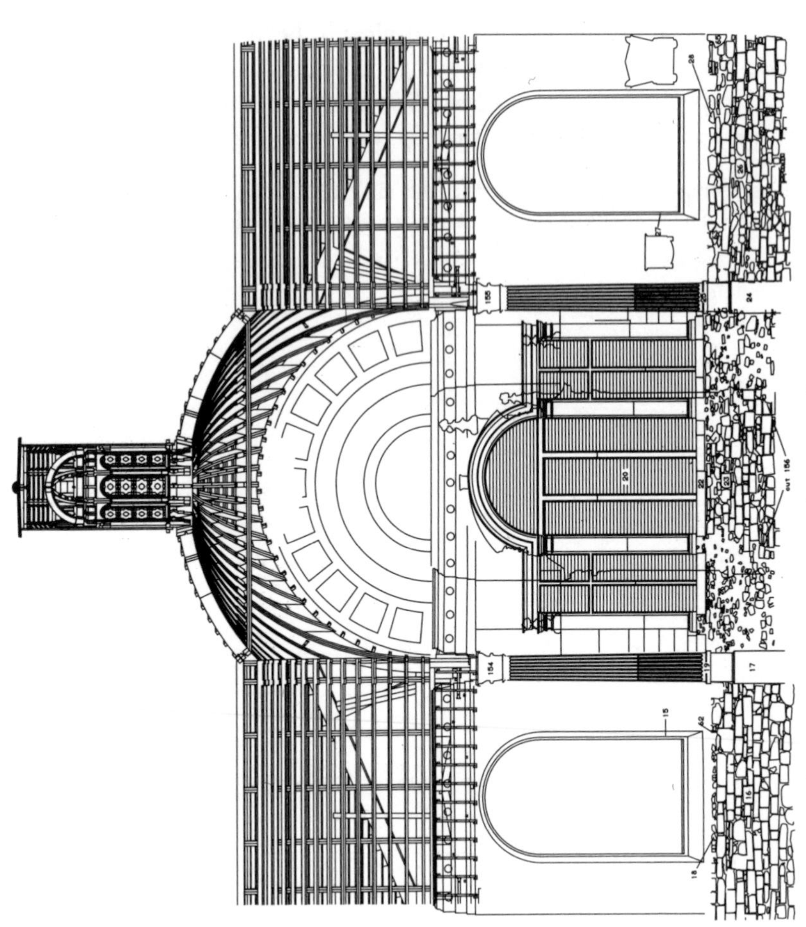

155
154
28
24
17
20
22
15
18
16

Fig. R11 The interior of the east end after Savage's rebuilding (1826–7)

The rebuilding of the church under Savage's supervision was a re-ordering of the interior space as a fully developed Greek cross plan (*see pages 23–27*). The mix of medieval and classical spatial values was swept away. The centre window had already been blocked in the eighteenth century by the reredos. The pilasters against the east wall were given fluted shafts to match the four columns in the centre of the church. The bases for these shafts were set higher than the originals, presumably to allow for a reordering of the panelling. The most significant alteration, however, was the complete replacement of the roof. Savage's intersecting round arched barrel vaults and spherical dome were much taller than Wren's coved ceiling. At the east end, it was possible to insert a 'D' shaped window above the reredos.

The interior was recorded in photographs from before the fire. The drawing of the roof in the reconstruction of the roof and lantern is based on the fire damaged timbers removed from the site in 1988.

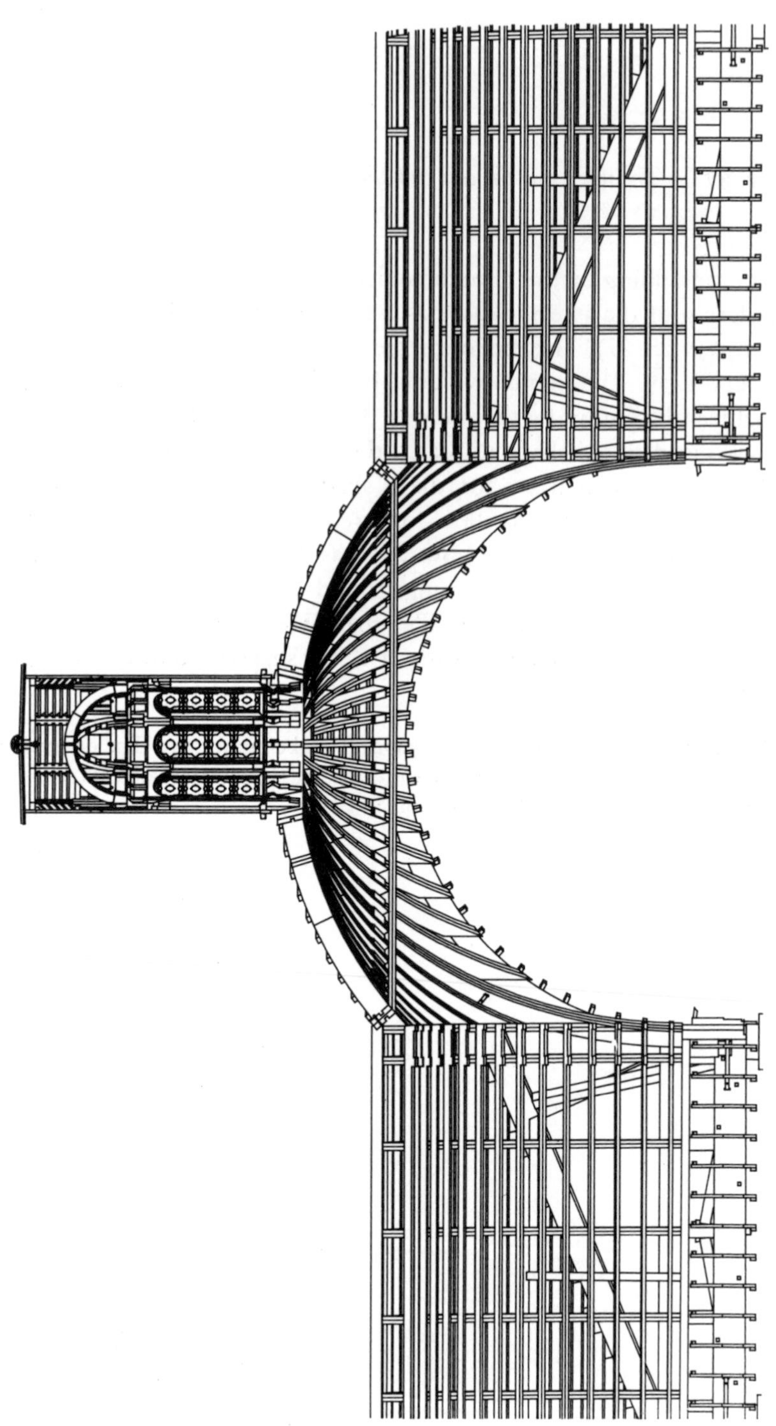

Fig. R12 The roof after Savage's rebuilding (1826-7)

As part of a major programme of rebuilding, Savage built a new roof, which survived until the fire of 1988. This drawing is based on a survey of the surviving timbers. (*See page 23*.)

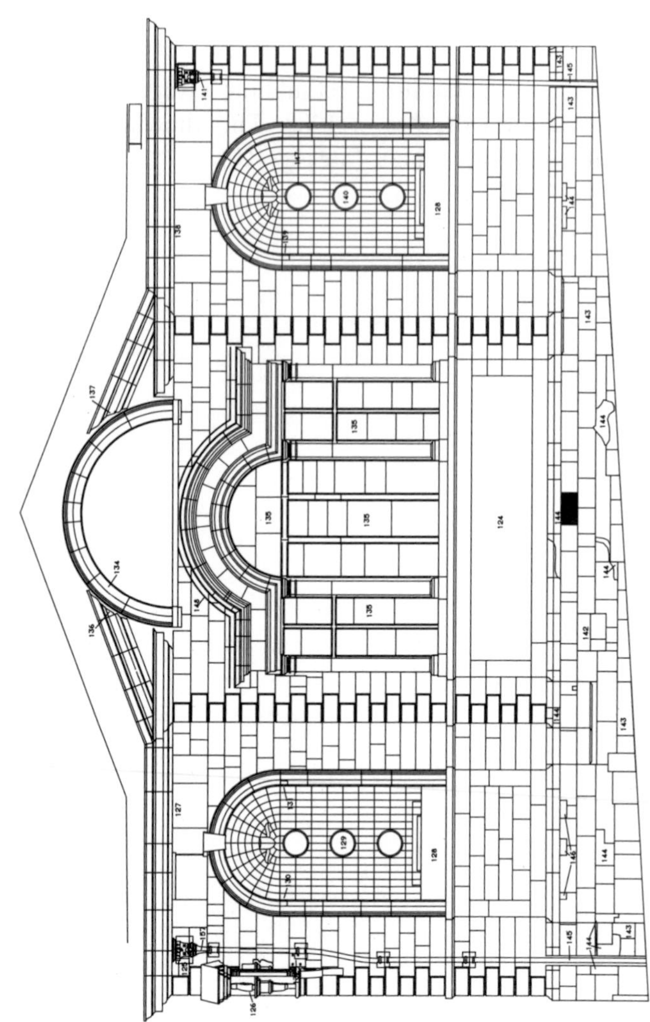

Fig. R13 The exterior of the east end (recent)

This drawing records the jointing in the ashlar and the detailing of the east front during the programme of repairs following the fire of 1988.

ST MARY-AT-HILL, FROM EASTCHEAP